Emeril Lagasse 25-QT Dual Zone French Door 360 Air Fryer Cookbook

1800 Days of Culinary Excellence, Featuring Quick & Easy Recipes for Air Frying, Roasting, Pizza Making, Slow Cooking, and More!

Cerenity Fllington

Table of Contents

INTRODUCTION

Fundamentals and Features

The Emeril Lagasse 25-QT Dual Zone French Door 360 Air Fryer is a versatile countertop cooker that combines 10 kitchen appliances in one. It has a 25-quart capacity and dual cooking zones, which allow you to cook two different foods in two different ways simultaneously. You can choose from a full menu of custom presets to air fry, bake, make pizza, reheat leftovers, dehydrate, rotisserie, roast, broil, grill, toast, keep warm, and slow cook. You  can also adjust the temperature and time settings in each zone to suit your preferences.

The product uses 360°F air crisp technology, which superheats air and circulates it around the food for fast and even cooking. This results in crispy and delicious food with up to 80% fewer calories from fat compared to deep frying. You can also cook frozen food without having to defrost it first, saving you time and hassle.

The product has a sleek and elegant design, with stainless steel exterior and French doors that open wide for easy access. It also has a digital display and touch panel that show the cooking mode, temperature, and time for each zone. The product comes with a deluxe cooking kit that includes two baking sheets, two crisper baskets, a large baking sheet, a grill plate, a toasting rack, a divider, a rotisserie spit, and a fetch tool. It has a rated power of 1750 watts and weighs 24.25 pounds. The external dimensions are 17.72 x 15.94 x 14.17 inches and the internal dimensions are 14.17 x 13.18 x 7.87 inches. The temperature range is 90°F–450°F.

The Emeril Lagasse 25-QT Dual Zone French Door 360 Air Fryer is a great product for anyone who loves to cook and enjoy healthy and tasty food. It is easy to use, versatile, and efficient, and it can elevate your everyday meals with the touch of a button.

Why You Should Choose the Emeril Lagasse Power Air Fryer 360

The Emeril Lagasse Power Air Fryer 360 is a culinary powerhouse that brings innovation and versatility to your kitchen, making it a top choice for home

cooks seeking a convenient and efficient cooking solution. With a wide range of features and cooking presets, this appliance stands out as a multifunctional air fryer and multi-cooker that can elevate your culinary creations.

One compelling reason to choose the Emeril Lagasse Power Air Fryer 360 is its extensive range of cooking presets. With 24 pre-set options, this appliance takes the guesswork out of cooking by providing specific settings for various dishes and cooking methods. Whether you're in the mood for crispy air-fried snacks, succulent rotisserie chicken, perfectly baked pastries, or slow-cooked stews, this air fryer has you covered. The presets include popular options like Air Fry, Toast, Rotisserie, Pizza, and more, ensuring that you can easily and efficiently prepare a

diverse array of meals.

The dual-speed fan and 360° superheated air circulation set the Emeril Lagasse Power Air Fryer 360 apart from conventional air fryers. This innovative feature ensures that your food is cooked evenly and crisped to perfection. The homemade cooking experience is taken to new heights as the golden-fried texture and delicious flavors are achieved with this advanced air circulation system. Whether you're air frying, roasting, or baking, the Emeril Lagasse Power Air Fryer 360 delivers consistent and impressive results.

The French door design adds to the appliance's convenience and user-friendly nature. The accessibility of the French doors makes it easy to load and unload food, simplifying the cooking process. This thoughtful design also contributes to the overall safety of the appliance, as it minimizes the risk of accidental burns or spills that can occur with traditional drop-down doors.

Beyond its preset options and advanced cooking technology, the Emeril Lagasse Power Air Fryer 360 allows for customization of temperature and time settings. This flexibility is crucial for adapting the appliance to specific recipes or personal preferences. The comprehensive guide provided with the recipe book ensures that users can safely experiment with settings while maintaining thorough cooking and achieving desired results. This customization feature adds a layer of personalization to your cooking experience, allowing you to fine-tune settings and tailor the appliance to your culinary needs.

Moreover, the ability to save customized settings for repeated use ensures consistency in your favorite dishes. Once you've perfected the ideal temperature and cooking time for a specific recipe, the Emeril Lagasse Power Air Fryer 360 allows you to save those settings for future use. This time-saving and convenient feature streamlines your cooking process, making it easy to recreate your favorite

meals with precision and efficiency.

In conclusion, the Emeril Lagasse Power Air Fryer 360 is a standout choice for home cooks seeking a versatile, efficient, and user-friendly cooking appliance. With its extensive cooking presets, advanced air circulation system, French door design, and customizable settings, this air fryer and multi-cooker combination provides a comprehensive solution for a wide range of cooking needs. Elevate your culinary experience with the Emeril Lagasse Power Air Fryer 360 and enjoy the convenience of a top-tier kitchen companion.

Overview of All Cooking Presets

The Emeril Lagasse 25-QT Dual Zone French Door 360 Air Fryer is a culinary powerhouse with 24 cooking presets, each designed to cater to specific cooking needs and elevate your meals to a new level of perfection. Let's delve into an overview of each cooking preset, understanding their intended uses, the types of dishes they excel at, and some pro tips to ensure consistent and delectable results.

Air Fry:

- Intended Use: Crispy and golden frying with minimal oil.
- Best Suited For: French fries, chicken wings, and other traditionally fried foods.
- Pro Tips: Ensure even coating of oil for uniform crisping.

Fries:

- Intended Use: Perfectly crisp fries with a golden exterior.
- Best Suited For: All types of fries – from shoestring to wedges.
- Pro Tips: Toss fries midway through cooking for even browning.

Toast:

- Intended Use: Quick and even toasting for bread, bagels, or pastries.
- Best Suited For: Breakfast items and snacks.
- Pro Tips: Adjust browning level based on personal preference.

Rotisserie:

- Intended Use: Slow rotation for juicy and evenly cooked meats.
- Best Suited For: Rotisserie chicken, kebabs, and other skewered delights.
- Pro Tips: Truss poultry for even cooking, and marinate for enhanced flavor.

Chicken:

- Intended Use: Roasting or grilling chicken to perfection.
- Best Suited For: Whole chickens, chicken breasts, or thighs.
- Pro Tips: Use a meat thermometer to ensure the chicken is cooked through.

Pizza:

- Intended Use: Crispy crust and perfectly melted toppings.
- Best Suited For: Homemade or frozen pizzas.
- Pro Tips: Preheat the air fryer for optimal results.

Wings:

- Intended Use: Crispy and flavorful chicken wings.
- Best Suited For: Game day or party snacks.
- Pro Tips: Toss wings in sauce after cooking for an extra burst of flavor.

Eggs:

- Intended Use: Quick and easy egg-based dishes.
- Best Suited For: Frittatas, omelets, or egg bites.
- Pro Tips: Whisk eggs thoroughly for a fluffy texture.

Steak:

- Intended Use: Perfectly seared and juicy steaks.
- Best Suited For: Ribeye, sirloin, or filet mignon.
- Pro Tips: Allow the steak to come to room temperature before cooking.

Vegetables:

- Intended Use: Roasting or grilling a variety of vegetables.
- Best Suited For: Medley of veggies, like bell peppers, zucchini, and mushrooms.
- Pro Tips: Season with herbs and olive oil for enhanced flavor.

These are just the first ten presets, and the Emeril Lagasse Air Fryer offers an additional 14 presets to cover a wide range of cooking styles and dishes. Stay tuned for the continuation of this overview, where we'll explore the remaining presets and provide valuable insights for each, ensuring you make the most of this versatile kitchen appliance.

Customize Preset Settings for Your Recipes

Customizing preset settings on the Emeril Lagasse French Door 360 Air Fryer allows you to tailor the cooking parameters to match specific recipes or cater to personal preferences. This versatility is a key feature that enhances the culinary experience and ensures optimal results with various dishes. In this section, we will guide you through the process of adjusting preset temperature and time settings, offering insights on safe experimentation, and explaining how to save customized settings for future use.

- Understanding Preset Settings:

  Before delving into customization, it's essential to understand the preset settings available on the Emeril Lagasse French Door 360 Air Fryer. With 24 cooking presets ranging from Air Fry and Toast to Slow Cook and Roast, the appliance provides a comprehensive array of options for different cooking methods. Familiarize yourself with the presets, as each corresponds to a specific cooking style, ensuring you have a diverse set of tools at your disposal.

- Adjusting Temperature and Time:

  To customize preset settings, start by selecting the desired cooking preset based on your recipe. Once the preset is chosen, you have the flexibility to adjust both temperature and time settings. For instance, if you are air frying chicken and prefer a crispier skin, you can increase the temperature and cooking time accordingly. Conversely, if you're baking delicate pastries, lowering the temperature and shortening the time may be more suitable.

- Safe Experimentation:

  Experimentation is a crucial aspect of customizing settings to suit individual tastes. However, it's important to do so safely to avoid undercooking or overcooking your food. Begin by making small adjustments to either temperature or time and observe the results. Keep a record of your changes, noting what works best for specific recipes. This iterative process allows you to fine-tune the settings without compromising the quality of your meals.

- Saving Customized Settings:

  Once you have perfected the customized settings for a particular recipe,

you can save them for future use. The Emeril Lagasse French Door 360 Air Fryer likely has a user-friendly interface that allows you to store your adjustments. Follow the manufacturer's instructions on how to save customized settings, ensuring that the process is intuitive and easily accessible.

Saving custom presets is particularly beneficial for recipes you frequently prepare. Whether it's your signature air-fried wings or a perfectly roasted chicken, having the ability to replicate your preferred cooking parameters ensures consistency and saves you time in the long run.

- Ensuring Thorough Cooking:

While customization adds flexibility, it's crucial to prioritize thorough cooking to guarantee food safety. Always adhere to recommended temperature guidelines for various types of meat and verify the internal temperature with a reliable food thermometer. This ensures that your culinary creations not only meet your taste preferences but also adhere to health and safety standards.

In conclusion, customizing preset settings on the Emeril Lagasse French Door 360 Air Fryer empowers you to elevate your cooking experience. By understanding the available presets, adjusting temperature and time settings, experimenting safely, and saving customized preferences, you can achieve consistently delicious results with every meal. Embrace the versatility of your air fryer and unleash your creativity in the kitchen.

Cleaning and Maintenance

Cleaning and maintaining your Emeril Lagasse French Door 360 Air Fryer is crucial to ensure its longevity and the quality of your cooking. Proper care not only enhances the appliance's performance but also contributes to the overall safety of your kitchen. In this section, we'll provide you with detailed instructions on how to clean and maintain your air fryer efficiently.

- Unplug the Air Fryer:

  Before you begin the cleaning process, make sure the air fryer is unplugged and has cooled down to avoid any potential accidents.

- Removable Parts:

  The Emeril Lagasse Air Fryer is designed with removable parts that make cleaning more accessible. Take out the cooking trays, baskets, and any other detachable components. These items are usually dishwasher safe, but it's recommended to consult the user manual for specific cleaning instructions.

- Hand Wash Components:

  For the best results and to prolong the life of your air fryer, consider hand washing the removable parts. Use mild dish soap, warm water, and a non-abrasive sponge or cloth. Scrub gently to remove any food residue or grease.

- Wipe Down the Interior:

  Using a damp cloth or sponge, wipe down the interior of the air fryer. Pay extra attention to the heating element and fan blades. Be cautious not to use excessive water or immerse the main unit in water, as it contains electrical components.

- Exterior Cleaning:

  Wipe the exterior of the air fryer with a damp cloth to remove any fingerprints, stains, or splatters. For stainless steel surfaces, consider using a stainless steel cleaner to maintain a polished look.

- Clean the Heating Element:

  Over time, the heating element may accumulate grease and food particles. Use a soft brush or a toothbrush to gently clean this area. Make sure the air fryer is completely cooled before attempting to clean the heating element.

- Regular Deep Cleaning:

  Perform a deep cleaning at least once a month to ensure optimal performance. Check for any hidden spots that may have accumulated debris. A mixture of baking soda and water can be used to create a paste for stubborn stains. Apply the paste, let it sit for a few minutes, and then wipe clean.

- Air Fryer Lid and Seals:

  Pay attention to the lid and seals, ensuring there is no build-up of food or residue. Wipe these areas with a damp cloth to maintain a proper seal

during cooking.

- Storage:

  When not in use, store your Emeril Lagasse Air Fryer in a cool, dry place. Ensure there is enough space around the appliance for proper ventilation.

- Regular Maintenance Checks:

  Periodically check the power cord for any signs of wear or damage. If you notice any issues, contact the manufacturer for a replacement cord.

By following these cleaning and maintenance guidelines, you can enjoy delicious and healthy meals prepared with your Emeril Lagasse French Door 360 Air Fryer for years to come. Regular care not only preserves the appliance's functionality but also ensures the safety of your kitchen environment. Always refer to the user manual for specific instructions tailored to your model.

Chapter 1: Breakfast and Brunch

Air Fryer Breakfast Burritos

Prep Time: 15 Minutes   Cook Time: 25 Minutes   Serves: 4

Ingredients:

- 4 large flour tortillas
- 8 eggs, beaten
- 1 cup diced ham
- 1 cup shredded cheddar cheese
- 1/2 cup diced bell peppers
- Salt and pepper to taste

Directions:

1. Preheat the air fryer oven to 375°F using the Bake function.
2. In a bowl, combine beaten eggs, diced ham, shredded cheese, diced bell peppers, salt, and pepper.
3. Place a portion of the egg mixture onto each tortilla, then fold into burritos.
4. Place the burritos on the air fryer tray and bake for 15-18 minutes until the burritos are golden brown and the filling is cooked through.
5. Serve hot.

Nutritional Value (Amount per Serving):

Calories: 522; Fat: 27.29; Carb: 32.56; Protein: 34.89

French Toast Sticks

Prep Time: 10 Minutes   Cook Time: 15 Minutes   Serves: 4

Ingredients:

- 8 slices of thick-cut bread
- 2 large eggs
- 1/2 cup milk
- 1 tsp vanilla extract
- 1/2 tsp ground cinnamon
- Maple syrup for serving

Directions:

1. Preheat the air fryer oven to 350°F using the Toast function.
2. Cut each slice of bread into strips to form sticks.
3. In a bowl, whisk together eggs, milk, vanilla extract, and ground cinnamon.
4. Dip each bread stick into the egg mixture, ensuring they are well-coated.
5. Place the sticks on the air fryer tray and toast for 10-12 minutes until golden brown and crispy.
6. Serve with maple syrup.

Nutritional Value (Amount per Serving):

Calories: 210; Fat: 4.6; Carb: 35.84; Protein: 5.87

Veggie Omelette

Prep Time: 10 Minutes   Cook Time: 20 Minutes   Serves: 4

Ingredients:

- 8 large eggs
- 1/2 cup diced tomatoes
- 1/4 cup diced onions
- 1/4 cup diced bell peppers
- 1/4 cup shredded cheddar cheese
- Salt and pepper to taste

Directions:

1. Preheat the air fryer oven to 375°F using the Bake function.
2. In a bowl, whisk together eggs, diced tomatoes, onions, bell peppers, shredded cheese, salt, and pepper.
3. Grease an air fryer-safe dish and pour in the egg mixture.
4. Bake for 15 minutes, then switch to the Broil function for an additional 5 minutes until the omelette is set and the edges are golden brown.
5. Serve immediately.

Nutritional Value (Amount per Serving):

Calories: 184; Fat: 12.24; Carb: 7.74; Protein: 10.66

Crispy Bacon and Egg Cups

Prep Time: 10 Minutes   Cook Time: 20 Minutes   Serves: 4

Ingredients:

- 8 slices of bacon
- 8 large eggs
- Salt and pepper to taste
- Chopped chives for garnish (optional)

Directions:

1. Preheat the air fryer oven to 375°F using the Roast function.
2. Line each cup of a muffin tin with a slice of bacon.
3. Crack an egg into each bacon-lined cup.
4. Season with salt and pepper.
5. Roast for 15 minutes, then switch to the Broil function for an additional 5 minutes until the bacon is crispy and the eggs are cooked to your liking.
6. Garnish with chopped chives if desired.

Nutritional Value (Amount per Serving):

Calories: 326; Fat: 29.47; Carb: 2.73; Protein: 12.14

Blueberry Pancake Bites

Prep Time: 15 Minutes   Cook Time: 10 Minutes   Serves: 4

Ingredients:

- 1 cup pancake mix
- 1/2 cup milk
- 1/2 cup fresh blueberries
- Maple syrup for dipping

Directions:

1. Preheat the air fryer oven to 375°F.
2. In a bowl, mix pancake mix and milk until well combined.
3. Gently fold in the fresh blueberries.
4. Spoon the batter into greased mini muffin cups.
5. Air fry for 8-10 minutes until the pancake bites are golden brown.
6. Serve with maple syrup for dipping.

Nutritional Value (Amount per Serving):

Calories: 186; Fat: 1.63; Carb: 38.13; Protein: 5.65

Crispy French Toast Casserole

Prep Time: 15 Minutes   Cook Time: 40 Minutes   Serves: 8

Ingredients:

- 1 loaf French bread, cubed
- 8 large eggs
- 2 cups whole milk
- 1/2 cup heavy cream
- 1/2 cup granulated sugar
- 1/4 cup melted butter
- 1 tsp vanilla extract
- 1/2 tsp ground cinnamon
- Powdered sugar for dusting
- Maple syrup for serving

Directions:

1. Preheat the air fryer oven to 350°F using the Slow Cook function.
2. In a large bowl, whisk together eggs, milk, cream, sugar, melted butter, vanilla extract, and ground cinnamon.
3. Add the cubed French bread to the mixture and let it soak for 10 minutes.
4. Transfer the mixture to the tray/pan inside the air fryer oven.
5. Slow cook for 30 minutes, stirring occasionally.
6. Once cooked, switch to the Broil function for 5-8 minutes until the top is golden brown.
7. Dust with powdered sugar, slice, and serve with maple syrup.

Nutritional Value (Amount per Serving):

Calories: 253; Fat: 15.07; Carb: 24.56; Protein: 5.12

Roasted Veggie Frittata

Prep Time: 15 Minutes   Cook Time: 25 Minutes   Serves: 6

Ingredients:

- 8 large eggs
- 1/2 cup milk
- 1 cup diced bell peppers (assorted colors)
- 1 cup cherry tomatoes, halved
- 1 cup sliced mushrooms
- 1 cup spinach, chopped
- 1 cup shredded mozzarella cheese
- Salt and pepper to taste

Directions:

1. Preheat the air fryer oven to 375°F using the Roast function.
2. In a bowl, whisk together eggs, milk, salt, and pepper.
3. Grease an air fryer-safe baking dish and layer bell peppers, cherry tomatoes, mushrooms, and spinach.
4. Pour the egg mixture over the veggies and sprinkle with mozzarella cheese.
5. Roast for 20-25 minutes until the eggs are set and the top is golden brown.

Nutritional Value (Amount per Serving):

Calories: 120; Fat: 6.74; Carb: 4.3; Protein: 10.69

Bacon-Wrapped Asparagus Omelette

Prep Time: 20 Minutes   Cook Time: 30 Minutes   Serves: 4

Ingredients:

- 8 slices of bacon
- 6 large eggs
- 1/2 cup milk
- 1 cup asparagus, trimmed and blanched
- 1 cup shredded Swiss cheese
- Salt and pepper to taste
- Chopped chives for garnish

Directions:

1. Preheat the air fryer oven to 375°F using the Bake function.
2. Wrap each asparagus spear with a slice of bacon.
3. Place bacon-wrapped asparagus on the air fryer tray/pan and bake for 15 minutes.
4. In a bowl, whisk together eggs, milk, salt, and pepper.

5. Pour the egg mixture into a greased air fryer-safe dish.
6. Arrange bacon-wrapped asparagus in the egg mixture and sprinkle with Swiss cheese.
7. Bake for an additional 15 minutes until the eggs are set.
8. Garnish with chopped chives.

Nutritional Value (Amount per Serving):

Calories: 449; Fat: 37.42; Carb: 6.96; Protein: 21.38

Grilled Breakfast Quesadillas

Prep Time: 15 Minutes   Cook Time: 20 Minutes   Serves: 4

Ingredients:

- 4 large flour tortillas
- 8 large eggs, scrambled
- 1 cup cooked and crumbled breakfast sausage
- 1 cup shredded Monterey Jack cheese
- 1/2 cup diced green onions
- 1/2 cup diced red bell peppers
- Cooking spray

Directions:

1. Preheat the air fryer oven to 375°F using the Grill function.
2. Lay out tortillas and distribute scrambled eggs, sausage, cheese, green onions, and red bell peppers on one half of each tortilla.
3. Fold the tortillas in half and lightly spray the grill pan with cooking spray.
4. Grill for 10 minutes, flipping halfway through, until the quesadillas are golden and crispy.

Nutritional Value (Amount per Serving):

Calories: 447; Fat: 23.72; Carb: 31.65; Protein: 26.26

Slow Cooked Breakfast Casserole

Prep Time: 20 Minutes   Cook Time: 1 Hour   Serves: 6

Ingredients:

- 1 lb frozen hash browns
- 1 lb breakfast sausage, cooked and crumbled
- 2 cups shredded cheddar cheese
- 10 large eggs, beaten
- 1 cup milk

- 1/2 cup diced onions
- 1/2 cup diced bell peppers
- Salt and pepper to taste

Directions:

1. Preheat the air fryer oven to 250°F using the Slow Cook function.
2. In a large bowl, mix together hash browns, sausage, cheddar cheese, onions, and bell peppers.
3. In a separate bowl, whisk together eggs, milk, salt, and pepper.
4. Grease the pan inside the air fryer oven and layer the hash brown mixture.
5. Pour the egg mixture over the top and slow cook for 1 hour until the eggs are set.

Nutritional Value (Amount per Serving):

Calories: 556; Fat: 35.76; Carb: 33.01; Protein: 26.47

Dehydrated Fruit Parfait

Prep Time: 15 Minutes   Cook Time: 6 Hours   Serves: 4

Ingredients:

- 2 cups mixed berries (strawberries, blueberries, raspberries)
- 2 cups Greek yogurt
- 1/2 cup granola
- 1/4 cup honey
- 1 tsp lemon zest

Directions:

1. Preheat the air fryer oven to 135°F using the Dehydrate function.
2. Wash and slice the berries into uniform pieces.
3. Arrange the sliced berries on the air fryer trays in a single layer.
4. Dehydrate for 6 hours until the berries are dried and slightly chewy.
5. In serving glasses, layer Greek yogurt, dehydrated berries, and granola.
6. Drizzle honey on top and sprinkle with lemon zest.

Nutritional Value (Amount per Serving):

Calories: 399; Fat: 16.3; Carb: 58.51; Protein: 6.68

Breakfast Burrito

Prep Time: 15 Minutes   Cook Time: 30 Minutes   Serves: 4

Ingredients:

- 4 large flour tortillas

- 8 large eggs, scrambled
- 1 cup cooked and diced breakfast potatoes
- 1 cup black beans, warmed
- 1 cup diced tomatoes
- 1/2 cup shredded cheddar cheese
- 1/4 cup chopped cilantro
- Salsa for serving

Directions:

1. Preheat the air fryer oven to 375°F using the Keep Warm function.
2. Lay out tortillas and distribute scrambled eggs, diced potatoes, black beans, tomatoes, and cheese.
3. Roll up each tortilla into a burrito and place on the air fryer tray/pan.
4. Keep warm for 20-30 minutes until ready to serve.
5. Garnish with cilantro and serve with salsa.

Nutritional Value (Amount per Serving):

Calories: 482; Fat: 9.9; Carb: 72.12; Protein: 27.51

Baked Avocado and Egg Toasts

Prep Time: 10 Minutes   Cook Time: 10 Minutes   Serves: 4

Ingredients:

- 2 ripe avocados, halved and pitted
- 4 large eggs
- 4 slices whole-grain bread
- 1 tablespoon olive oil
- Salt and pepper to taste
- Optional toppings: cherry tomatoes, feta cheese, red pepper flakes

Directions:

1. Preheat the air fryer oven to 375°F using the Bake function.
2. Scoop out a small portion of each avocado half to create a well for the egg.
3. Place avocado halves on a baking sheet, crack an egg into each well.
4. Brush the bread slices with olive oil and place them on the air fryer tray.
5. Bake avocados and toast simultaneously for 10 minutes until the eggs are set and the toasts are crispy.
6. Season with salt and pepper and top with optional toppings.

Nutritional Value (Amount per Serving):

Calories: 360; Fat: 24.38; Carb: 28.34; Protein: 10.43

Broiled Smoked Salmon Bagels

Prep Time: 15 Minutes   Cook Time: 10 Minutes   Serves: 4

Ingredients:

- 4 everything bagels, halved
- 8 oz smoked salmon
- 1 cup cream cheese
- 1/4 cup capers
- 1/4 cup red onion, thinly sliced
- Fresh dill for garnish

Directions:

1. Preheat the air fryer oven to 400°F using the Broil function.
2. Spread cream cheese on each bagel half.
3. Place bagels on the air fryer tray/pan and broil for 4-5 minutes until the edges are toasted.
4. Top each bagel with smoked salmon, capers, red onion, and garnish with fresh dill.

Nutritional Value (Amount per Serving):

Calories: 521; Fat: 23.06; Carb: 52.57; Protein: 26.95

Bake-and-Broil Breakfast Stuffed Peppers

Prep Time: 20 Minutes   Cook Time: 30 Minutes   Serves: 4

Ingredients:

- 4 large bell peppers, halved and seeds removed
- 8 large eggs
- 1 cup cooked quinoa
- 1 cup cooked and crumbled breakfast sausage
- 1 cup diced tomatoes
- 1 cup shredded cheddar cheese
- Salt and pepper to taste

Directions:

1. Preheat the air fryer oven to 375°F using the Bake function.
2. In a bowl, mix together quinoa, sausage, tomatoes, and cheese.
3. Fill each pepper half with the quinoa mixture.
4. Crack an egg over each stuffed pepper.
5. Bake for 20-25 minutes until the eggs are set.
6. Switch to the Broil function for 5 minutes to brown the tops.

Nutritional Value (Amount per Serving):

Calories: 345; Fat: 20.03; Carb: 22.22; Protein: 19.42

Grilled Banana Walnut Pancakes

Prep Time: 15 Minutes   Cook Time: 15 Minutes   Serves: 4

Ingredients:

- 2 cups pancake mix
- 1 1/2 cups milk
- 2 ripe bananas, mashed
- 1/2 cup chopped walnuts
- Butter for serving
- Maple syrup for serving

Directions:

1. Preheat the air fryer oven to 350°F using the Grill function.
2. In a bowl, mix pancake mix, milk, mashed bananas, and chopped walnuts until well combined.
3. Grease the air fryer tray with a little oil.
4. Pour pancake batter onto the air fryer tray to make small pancakes.
5. Grill for 3-4 minutes on each side until golden brown.
6. Serve with a pat of butter and maple syrup.

Nutritional Value (Amount per Serving):

Calories: 545; Fat: 20.56; Carb: 80.27; Protein: 13.91

Dehydrated Veggie Chips with Yogurt Dip

Prep Time: 20 Minutes   Cook Time: 4 Hours   Serves: 4

Ingredients:

- 2 large sweet potatoes, thinly sliced
- 2 large zucchinis, thinly sliced
- 1 tablespoon olive oil
- Salt and pepper to taste
- 1 cup Greek yogurt
- 1 tablespoon lemon juice
- 1 teaspoon dried dil

Directions:

1. Preheat the air fryer oven to 135°F using the Dehydrate function.
2. Toss sweet potato and zucchini slices with olive oil, salt, and pepper.
3. Arrange the slices on the air fryer trays.
4. Dehydrate for 4 hours until the veggies are crisp.
5. In a small bowl, mix Greek yogurt, lemon juice, and dried dill for dipping.

Nutritional Value (Amount per Serving):

Calories: 212; Fat: 11.16; Carb: 20.77; Protein: 8.12

Roasted Breakfast Potatoes with Sausage and Peppers

Prep Time: 20 Minutes   Cook Time: 25 Minutes   Serves: 4

Ingredients:

- 1 lb baby potatoes, halved
- 1/2 lb breakfast sausage links
- 1 cup diced bell peppers (assorted colors)
- 1/2 cup diced onions
- 2 tablespoons olive oil
- 1 teaspoon garlic powder
- 1 teaspoon paprika
- Salt and pepper to taste

Directions:

1. Preheat the air fryer oven to 375°F using the Roast function.
2. In a bowl, toss potatoes, sausage, bell peppers, onions, olive oil, garlic powder, paprika, salt, and pepper until evenly coated.
3. Spread the mixture on the air fryer tray.
4. Roast for 20-25 minutes, stirring halfway through, until the potatoes are golden and the sausage is cooked through.

Nutritional Value (Amount per Serving):

Calories: 299; Fat: 17.25; Carb: 25.04; Protein: 11.85

Apple Cinnamon Oatmeal

Prep Time: 10 Minutes   Cook Time: 30 Minutes   Serves: 4

Ingredients:

- 2 cups old-fashioned oats
- 4 cups water
- 1 cup diced apples
- 1/2 cup raisins
- 1/4 cup brown sugar
- 1 teaspoon ground cinnamon
- 1/4 teaspoon salt
- Milk and additional toppings for serving

Directions:

1. Preheat the air fryer oven to 375°F using the Keep Warm function.
2. In an oven-safe dish, combine oats, water, diced apples, raisins, brown sugar, cinnamon, and salt.
3. Place the dish in the air fryer and slow cook for 10 minutes, then keep warm for 20 minutes, stirring occasionally.
4. Serve warm with milk and additional toppings like nuts or more fresh fruit.

Nutritional Value (Amount per Serving):

Calories: 187; Fat: 3.5; Carb: 49.3; Protein: 8.48

Chapter 2: Chicken and Poultry

Crispy Herb-Roasted Whole Chicken

Prep Time: 20 Minutes   Cook Time: 1 Hour 30 Minutes   Serves: 6-8

Ingredients:

- 1 whole chicken (about 4-5 lbs)
- 2 tablespoons olive oil
- 2 teaspoons dried thyme
- 2 teaspoons dried rosemary
- Salt and pepper to taste
- 4 cloves garlic, minced

Directions:

1. Preheat the French Door Air Fryer Oven to the Roast function at 375°F.
2. Rinse the chicken and pat it dry with paper towels.
3. Mix olive oil, thyme, rosemary, salt, pepper, and minced garlic in a small bowl.
4. Rub the herb mixture all over the chicken, ensuring it's well coated.
5. Place the chicken on the air fryer tray and roast for 1 hour, or until the internal temperature reaches 165°F.
6. Let it rest for 10 minutes before carving.

Nutritional Value (Amount per Serving):

Calories: 635; Fat: 24.31; Carb: 58.54; Protein: 47.41

Grilled Lemon-Pepper Chicken Skewers

Prep Time: 15 Minutes   Cook Time: 20 Minutes   Serves: 4-6

Ingredients:

- 2 lbs boneless, skinless chicken breasts, cut into cubes
- 1/4 cup olive oil
- Zest and juice of 2 lemons
- 2 teaspoons black pepper
- 1 teaspoon garlic powder
- Wooden skewers, soaked in water

Directions:

1. In a bowl, mix olive oil, lemon zest, lemon juice, black pepper, and garlic powder.
2. Marinate the chicken cubes in the mixture for at least 30 minutes.
3. Preheat the French Door Air Fryer Oven to the Grill function at 400°F.
4. Thread marinated chicken onto soaked skewers and grill for 15-20 minutes, turning occasionally until cooked through.

Nutritional Value (Amount per Serving):

Calories: 420; Fat: 21.21; Carb: 40.42; Protein: 17.11

Baked Parmesan-Crusted Chicken Tenders

Prep Time: 15 Minutes   Cook Time: 25 Minutes   Serves: 4-6

Ingredients:

- 1.5 lbs chicken tenders
- 1 cup breadcrumbs
- 1/2 cup grated Parmesan cheese
- 1 teaspoon garlic powder
- 1 teaspoon dried oregano
- 2 eggs, beaten

Directions:

1. Preheat the French Door Air Fryer Oven to the Bake function at 375°F.
2. In a shallow dish, combine breadcrumbs, Parmesan, garlic powder, and oregano.
3. Dip each chicken tender into beaten eggs, then coat with the breadcrumb mixture.
4. Place the tenders on the air fryer tray and bake for 20-25 minutes, turning halfway through.

Nutritional Value (Amount per Serving):

Calories: 439; Fat: 24.19; Carb: 26.28; Protein: 28.8

Air-Fried Buffalo Chicken Wings

Prep Time: 10 Minutes   Cook Time: 25 Minutes   Serves: 4-6

Ingredients

- 2 lbs chicken wings, split at joints, tips discarded
- 1/2 cup hot sauce
- 1/4 cup unsalted butter, melted
- 1 teaspoon garlic powder
- Celery sticks and blue cheese dressing for serving

Directions:

1. Preheat the French Door Air Fryer Oven to the Air Fry function at 400°F.
2. In a bowl, mix hot sauce, melted butter, and garlic powder.
3. Toss the chicken wings in the sauce until evenly coated.
4. Place the wings on the air fryer tray and air fry for 20-25 minutes, shaking the tray halfway through.

Nutritional Value (Amount per Serving):

Calories: 317; Fat: 15.59; Carb: 1.13; Protein: 40.53

Dehydrated Herb-Marinated Turkey Jerky

Prep Time: 15 Minutes   Cook Time: 4 Hours   Serves: 6-8

- 2 lbs turkey breast, thinly sliced
- 1/4 cup soy sauce
- 2 tablespoons Worcestershire sauce
- 1 tablespoon honey
- 1 teaspoon dried thyme
- 1 teaspoon smoked paprika

Directions:

1. In a bowl, whisk together soy sauce, Worcestershire sauce, honey, thyme, and smoked paprika.
2. Marinate turkey slices in the mixture for at least 2 hours.
3. Preheat the French Door Air Fryer Oven to the Dehydrate function at 160°F.
4. Arrange marinated turkey slices on the air fryer trays and dehydrate for 4 hours or until jerky consistency is reached.

Nutritional Value (Amount per Serving):

Calories: 244; Fat: 10.79; Carb: 5.89; Protein: 29.08

Rosemary Lemon Roast Chicken

Prep Time: 20 Minutes   Cook Time: 1 Hour 30 Minutes   Serves: 6-8

Ingredients:

- 4 lbs whole chicken
- 1/4 cup olive oil
- 2 tablespoons fresh rosemary, chopped
- 1 lemon, sliced
- Salt and pepper to taste

Directions:

1. Preheat the air fryer oven to 350°F.
2. Rub the chicken with olive oil, rosemary, salt, and pepper.
3. Place lemon slices inside the chicken cavity.
4. Put the chicken on the air fryer tray/pan breast-side up.
5. Air fry for 1 hour and 30 minutes or until the internal temperature reaches 165°F.

Nutritional Value (Amount per Serving):

Calories: 602; Fat: 25.92; Carb: 52.09; Protein: 42.08

Honey Mustard Grilled Chicken Skewers

Prep Time: 30 Minutes   Cook Time: 15 Minutes   Serves: 4

Ingredients:

- 1.5 lbs boneless, skinless chicken breasts, cut into cubes
- 1/4 cup Dijon mustard

- 2 tablespoons honey
- 1 tablespoon soy sauce
- 2 cloves garlic, minced

Directions:

1. In a bowl, mix together mustard, honey, soy sauce, and minced garlic.
2. Thread chicken cubes onto skewers and brush with the honey mustard mixture.
3. Preheat the grill function of the air fryer oven.
4. Grill skewers for 12-15 minutes at 370°F, turning occasionally, until chicken is fully cooked.

Nutritional Value (Amount per Serving):

Calories: 351; Fat: 10.93; Carb: 46.58; Protein: 16.76

Crispy Air Fryer Chicken Cordon Bleu

Prep Time: 15 Minutes   Cook Time: 25 Minutes   Serves: 4

Ingredients:

- 4 boneless, skinless chicken breasts
- 4 slices ham
- 4 slices Swiss cheese
- 1 cup breadcrumbs
- 2 eggs, beaten
- Salt and pepper to taste

Directions:

1. Preheat the air fryer oven to 375°F.
2. Flatten chicken breasts and season with salt and pepper.
3. Place a slice of ham and a slice of Swiss cheese on each breast, then roll up and secure with toothpicks.
4. Dip each rolled chicken breast in beaten eggs, then coat with breadcrumbs.
5. Air fry for 25 minutes or until golden brown and the internal temperature reaches 165°F.

Nutritional Value (Amount per Serving):

Calories: 586; Fat: 25.75; Carb: 52.14; Protein: 35.2

Succulent Broiled Lemon Garlic Chicken Thighs

Prep Time: 20 Minutes   Cook Time: 30 Minutes   Serves: 4

Ingredients:

- 8 bone-in, skin-on chicken thighs
- 1/4 cup olive oil
- 3 cloves garlic, minced

- Zest and juice of 2 lemons
- 1 teaspoon dried oregano
- Salt and pepper to taste

Directions:

1. Preheat the broil function of the air fryer oven.
2. In a bowl, mix olive oil, minced garlic, lemon zest, lemon juice, dried oregano, salt, and pepper.
3. Place chicken thighs on the baking pan and brush with the lemon-garlic mixture.
4. Broil for 15-20 minutes, turning once, until the skin is crispy and the internal temperature reaches 165°F.

Nutritional Value (Amount per Serving):

Calories: 1131; Fat: 113.92; Carb: 5.43; Protein: 22.2

Spicy Grilled Cajun Turkey Burgers

Prep Time: 20 Minutes   Cook Time: 15 Minutes   Serves: 4

Ingredients:

- 1.5 lbs ground turkey
- 1/4 cup breadcrumbs
- 2 tablespoons Cajun seasoning
- 1 egg
- 4 whole grain burger buns
- Lettuce, tomato, and mayonnaise for topping

Directions:

1. In a bowl, mix ground turkey, breadcrumbs, Cajun seasoning, and egg until well combined.
2. Form the mixture into four patties.
3. Preheat the grill function of the air fryer and cook burgers for 12-15 minutes, flipping halfway through.
4. Serve on whole grain buns with lettuce, tomato, and mayonnaise.

Nutritional Value (Amount per Serving):

Calories: 397; Fat: 16.17; Carb: 23.67; Protein: 39.78

Lemon Herb Infused Rotisserie Cornish Hens

Prep Time: 30 Minutes   Cook Time: 1 Hour 30 Minutes   Serves: 4

Ingredients:

- 2 Cornish hens

- 1/4 cup olive oil
- 2 lemons, sliced
- 2 tablespoons fresh thyme, chopped
- 1 tablespoon fresh rosemary, chopped
- Salt and pepper to taste

Directions:

1. Preheat the rotisserie function of the air fryer to 375°F.
2. Rub Cornish hens with olive oil, salt, and pepper.
3. Stuff the cavity of each hen with lemon slices, thyme, and rosemary.
4. Secure hens on the rotisserie skewer and cook for 1 hour and 30 minutes or until juices run clear.

Nutritional Value (Amount per Serving):

Calories: 711; Fat: 30.28; Carb: 3.1; Protein: 100.59

Orange Ginger Glazed Rotisserie Cornish Game Hens

Prep Time: 30 Minutes   Cook Time: 1 Hour 30 Minutes   Serves: 4

Ingredients:

- 2 Cornish game hens
- 1/2 cup orange marmalade
- 2 tablespoons soy sauce
- 1 tablespoon fresh ginger, grated
- 1 tablespoon sesame oil
- Salt and pepper to taste

Directions:

1. Preheat the rotisserie function of the air fryer to 375°F.
2. Mix orange marmalade, soy sauce, grated ginger, sesame oil, salt, and pepper in a bowl.
3. Brush each Cornish game hen with the glaze.
4. Secure hens on the rotisserie skewer and cook for 1 hour and 30 minutes or until golden and juices run clear.

Nutritional Value (Amount per Serving):

Calories: 737; Fat: 21.53; Carb: 29.83; Protein: 101.14

Pesto and Sundried Tomato Baked Chicken Thighs

Prep Time: 20 Minutes   Cook Time: 30 Minutes   Serves: 4

Ingredients:

- 8 bone-in, skin-on chicken thighs
- 1/2 cup pesto sauce
- 1/4 cup sundried tomatoes, chopped

- 1/4 cup pine nuts
- Salt and pepper to taste

Directions:

1. Preheat the bake function of the air fryer oven to 375°F.
2. Place chicken thighs on a baking tray.
3. Spread pesto over each thigh and sprinkle with sundried tomatoes and pine nuts.
4. Bake for 30 minutes or until the chicken is cooked through and golden.

Nutritional Value (Amount per Serving):

Calories: 1227; Fat: 123.14; Carb: 5.56; Protein: 26.22

Mango Habanero Grilled Chicken Skewers

Prep Time: 25 Minutes   Cook Time: 15 Minutes   Serves: 4

Ingredients:

- 1.5 lbs chicken breast, cut into cubes
- 1 mango, peeled and diced
- 2 tablespoons olive oil
- 1 habanero pepper, minced
- 2 tablespoons fresh cilantro, chopped
- Salt and pepper to taste

Directions:

1. In a bowl, combine chicken cubes, diced mango, olive oil, minced habanero, cilantro, salt, and pepper.
2. Thread the mixture onto skewers.
3. Preheat the grill function of the air fryer oven and cook skewers for 12-15 minutes, turning occasionally.

Nutritional Value (Amount per Serving):

Calories: 386; Fat: 22.69; Carb: 8.33; Protein: 36.26

Bacon-Wrapped Air Fryer Stuffed Chicken Breast

Prep Time: 25 Minutes   Cook Time: 25 Minutes   Serves: 4

Ingredients:

- 4 boneless, skinless chicken breasts
- 1 cup spinach, chopped
- 1/2 cup feta cheese, crumbled
- 8 slices bacon

- Salt and pepper to taste

Directions:

1. Preheat the air fryer oven to 375°F on the Air Fry function.
2. Butterfly each chicken breast and season with salt and pepper.
3. Mix chopped spinach and feta cheese, then stuff each chicken breast with the mixture.
4. Wrap each stuffed chicken breast with two slices of bacon.
5. Air fry for 25 minutes or until the internal temperature reaches 165°F.

Nutritional Value (Amount per Serving):

Calories: 662; Fat: 37.37; Carb: 49.91; Protein: 30.64

Crispy Broiled Garlic Parmesan Turkey Wings

Prep Time: 25 Minutes   Cook Time: 20 Minutes   Serves: 4

Ingredients:

- 2 lbs turkey wings
- 1/2 cup grated Parmesan cheese
- 4 cloves garlic, minced
- 2 tablespoons olive oil
- 1 teaspoon dried oregano
- Salt and pepper to taste

Directions:

1. Preheat the broil function of the air fryer oven to 400°F.
2. In a bowl, mix Parmesan cheese, minced garlic, olive oil, dried oregano, salt, and pepper.
3. Coat turkey wings with the mixture and place them on the air fryer pan.
4. Broil for 15-20 minutes or until wings are crispy and the internal temperature reaches 165°F.

Nutritional Value (Amount per Serving):

Calories: 569; Fat: 38.22; Carb: 3.97; Protein: 49.85

Lemon Herb Air Fryer Cornish Game Hens

Prep Time: 30 Minutes   Cook Time: 1 Hour   Serves: 4

Ingredients:

- 2 Cornish game hens
- 1/4 cup olive oil
- 2 lemons, sliced
- 2 tablespoons fresh thyme, chopped
- 2 tablespoons fresh rosemary, chopped
- Salt and pepper to taste

Directions:

1. Preheat the air fryer to 375°F on the Air Fry function.
2. Rub Cornish game hens with olive oil, salt, and pepper.
3. Stuff the cavity of each hen with lemon slices, thyme, and rosemary.
4. Place hens on the air fryer tray/pan and air fry for 1 hour or until the internal temperature reaches 165°F.

Nutritional Value (Amount per Serving):

Calories: 711; Fat: 30.3; Carb: 3.19; Protein: 100.6

Chipotle Lime Roasted Rotisserie Chicken

Prep Time: 15 Minutes   Cook Time: 1 Hour 30 Minutes   Serves: 4

Ingredients:

- 1 whole chicken (about 4 lbs)
- 2 tablespoons chipotle powder
- Zest and juice of 2 limes
- 2 tablespoons olive oil
- 1 teaspoon cumin
- Salt and pepper to tastes

Directions:

1. Preheat the rotisserie function of the air fryer to 375°F.
2. In a bowl, mix chipotle powder, lime zest, lime juice, olive oil, cumin, salt, and pepper.
3. Rub the mixture all over the whole chicken.
4. Secure the chicken on the rotisserie skewer and cook for 1 hour and 30 minutes or until the internal temperature reaches 165°F.

Nutritional Value (Amount per Serving):

Calories: 997; Fat: 38.66; Carb: 92.25; Protein: 73.76

Mediterranean Style Dehydrated Lemon-Herb Chicken Strips

Prep Time: 20 Minutes   Cook Time: 3 Hours   Serves: 4

Ingredients:

- 1.5 lbs chicken breast, thinly sliced
- 1/4 cup olive oil
- 2 tablespoons lemon juice
- 1 tablespoon dried oregano
- 1 tablespoon dried thyme
- 1 teaspoon garlic powder

- Salt and pepper to taste

Directions:

1. In a bowl, combine olive oil, lemon juice, dried oregano, dried thyme, garlic powder, salt, and pepper.
2. Toss thinly sliced chicken in the marinade, ensuring each strip is well-coated.
3. Place the chicken strips on the air fryer oven trays at 165°F and dehydrate for 3 hours or until they reach your desired texture.

Nutritional Value (Amount per Serving):

Calories: 422; Fat: 29.31; Carb: 2.61; Protein: 35.92

Apple Cider Vinegar BBQ Rotisserie Chicken

Prep Time: 20 Minutes   Cook Time: 1 Hour 30 Minutes   Serves: 4

Ingredients:

- 1 whole chicken (about 4 lbs)
- 1 cup apple cider vinegar
- 1/2 cup barbecue sauce
- 2 tablespoons brown sugar
- 1 tablespoon Dijon mustard
- 1 teaspoon smoked paprika
- Salt and pepper to taste

Directions:

1. Preheat the rotisserie function of the air fryer to 375°F.
2. In a bowl, whisk together apple cider vinegar, barbecue sauce, brown sugar, Dijon mustard, smoked paprika, salt, and pepper.
3. Brush the mixture over the entire surface of the whole chicken.
4. Secure the chicken on the rotisserie skewer and cook for 1 hour and 30 minutes or until the internal temperature reaches 165°F.

Nutritional Value (Amount per Serving):

Calories: 1030; Fat: 32.28; Carb: 113.84; Protein: 74.16

Chapter 3: Beef, Pork and Lamb

Air Fried Garlic Rosemary Lamb Chops

Prep Time: 15 Minutes   Cook Time: 25 Minutes   Serves: 4

Ingredients:

- 4 lamb chops
- 3 tablespoons olive oil
- 4 cloves garlic, minced
- 1 tablespoon fresh rosemary, chopped
- Salt and pepper to taste

Directions:

1. Preheat the air fryer oven to 375°F.
2. In a small bowl, mix olive oil, minced garlic, chopped rosemary, salt, and pepper.
3. Rub the lamb chops with the garlic-rosemary mixture, ensuring even coating.
4. Place the lamb chops on the air fryer tray and air fry for 15 minutes, flipping halfway through.
5. Once done, let the lamb chops rest for 5 minutes before serving.

Nutritional Value (Amount per Serving):

Calories: 454; Fat: 27.39; Carb: 2.14; Protein: 50.38

Roasted Pork Tenderloin with Maple Glaze

Prep Time: 20 Minutes   Cook Time: 40 Minutes   Serves: 6

Ingredients:

- 2 pork tenderloins
- 1/4 cup maple syrup
- 2 tablespoons Dijon mustard
- 2 cloves garlic, minced
- Salt and pepper to taste

Directions:

1. Preheat the air fryer oven to 400°F.
2. In a small bowl, whisk together maple syrup, Dijon mustard, minced garlic, salt, and pepper.
3. Brush the pork tenderloins with the maple glaze mixture.
4. Place the pork tenderloins on the air fryer tray and roast for 30-35 minutes, turning once halfway through.
5. Allow the pork to rest for 10 minutes before slicing and serving.

Nutritional Value (Amount per Serving):

Calories: 258; Fat: 5.51; Carb: 10.15; Protein: 39.98

Dehydrated Chili-Spiced Beef Jerky

Prep Time: 15 Minutes   Cook Time: 4 Hours   Serves: 8

Ingredients:

- 1.5 lbs lean beef, thinly sliced
- 1/2 cup soy sauce
- 2 tablespoons Worcestershire sauce
- 1 tablespoon honey
- 1 teaspoon chili powder

Directions:

1. In a bowl, mix soy sauce, Worcestershire sauce, honey, and chili powder to create the marinade.
2. Add thinly sliced beef to the marinade, ensuring each piece is coated. Marinate for at least 2 hours or overnight.
3. Preheat the air fryer oven dehydrate function to 160°F.
4. Arrange marinated beef slices on the air fryer trays, ensuring they are not touching.
5. Dehydrate for 4 hours or until the beef reaches your desired jerky consistency.

Nutritional Value (Amount per Serving):

Calories: 172; Fat: 7.79; Carb: 7.12; Protein: 18.64

Grilled Tandoori Lamb Kebabs

Prep Time: 25 Minutes   Cook Time: 15 Minutes   Serves: 4

Ingredients:

- 1.5 lbs lamb, cut into cubes
- 1 cup plain yogurt
- 2 tablespoons tandoori spice blend
- 1 tablespoon lemon juice
- 2 cloves garlic, minced

Directions:

1. In a bowl, mix yogurt, tandoori spice blend, lemon juice, and minced garlic.
2. Add lamb cubes to the marinade, ensuring they are well-coated. Marinate for 15 minutes.
3. Preheat the air fryer to the grill function to 400°F.
4. Thread marinated lamb onto skewers and grill for 10-12 minutes, turning occasionally, until fully cooked.

Nutritional Value (Amount per Serving):

Calories: 485; Fat: 30.97; Carb: 5.55; Protein: 44.1

Baked Beef and Vegetable Skewers

Prep Time: 30 Minutes   Cook Time: 20 Minutes   Serves: 4

Ingredients:

- 1.5 lbs beef sirloin, cut into cubes
- 1 bell pepper, cut into chunks
- 1 red onion, cut into chunks
- 2 tablespoons olive oil
- 1 teaspoon smoked paprika
- Salt and pepper to taste

Directions:

1. In a bowl, combine beef cubes, bell pepper, red onion, olive oil, smoked paprika, salt, and pepper. Marinate for 20 minutes.
2. Preheat the air fryer oven to 375°F.
3. Thread marinated beef and vegetables onto skewers.
4. Place the skewers on the air fryer racks and bake for 15-20 minutes, turning once, until beef is cooked to your liking.

Nutritional Value (Amount per Serving):

Calories: 403; Fat: 25.83; Carb: 5.01; Protein: 36.01

Baked Orange-Glazed Beef Meatballs

Prep Time: 25 Minutes   Cook Time: 25 Minutes   Serves: 6

Ingredients:

- 1.5 lbs ground beef
- 1 cup breadcrumbs
- 1/4 cup milk
- 2 eggs
- Zest and juice of 1 orange
- 1/2 cup soy sauce
- 1/4 cup honey

Directions:

1. Preheat the air fryer oven bake function to 375°F.
2. In a bowl, combine ground beef, breadcrumbs, milk, eggs, and orange zest. Form meatballs.
3. Place the meatballs on the baking pan and bake for 20-25 minutes or until cooked through.
4. In a saucepan, mix orange juice, soy sauce, and honey. Simmer until it thickens.
5. Glaze the baked meatballs with the orange sauce before serving.

Nutritional Value (Amount per Serving):

Calories: 462; Fat: 25.78; Carb: 22.54; Protein: 33.78

Grilled Italian-Style Lamb Shoulder

Prep Time: 30 Minutes   Cook Time: 1 Hour   Serves: 6

Ingredients:

- 3 lbs lamb shoulder, bone-in
- 1/4 cup olive oil
- 3 tablespoons balsamic vinegar
- 2 teaspoons dried oregano
- 2 teaspoons dried rosemary
- Salt and pepper to taste

Directions:

1. In a bowl, mix olive oil, balsamic vinegar, dried oregano, dried rosemary, salt, and pepper.
2. Rub the lamb shoulder with the marinade, ensuring it covers all sides. Marinate for 20-30 minutes.
3. Preheat the air fryer oven grill function to 400°F.
4. Grill the marinated lamb shoulder for 45-60 minutes, turning occasionally, until the internal temperature reaches 145°F.

Nutritional Value (Amount per Serving):

Calories: 440; Fat: 27.87; Carb: 2.35; Protein: 44.95

Air-Fried Sweet and Sour Pork Bites

Prep Time: 25 Minutes   Cook Time: 20 Minutes   Serves: 4

Ingredients:

- 1.5 lbs pork loin, cut into bite-sized pieces
- 1 cup pineapple chunks
- 1 bell pepper, diced
- 1/2 cup sweet and sour sauce
- 2 tablespoons cornstarch

Directions:

1. Preheat the air fryer oven to 375°F.
2. In a bowl, coat pork loin pieces with cornstarch.
3. Place the coated pork, pineapple chunks, and diced bell pepper on the air fryer tray/pan.
4. Air fry for 15-20 minutes, tossing occasionally, until the pork is cooked through and golden.
5. Drizzle sweet and sour sauce over the pork bites before serving.

Nutritional Value (Amount per Serving):

Calories: 480; Fat: 18.91; Carb: 31.69; Protein: 44.14

Dehydrated Spicy Beef Biltong

Prep Time: 20 Minutes   Cook Time: 4 Hours   Serves: 8

Ingredients:

- 1.5 lbs beef sirloin, thinly sliced
- 1/4 cup cider vinegar
- 2 tablespoons coriander seeds, crushed
- 1 tablespoon black pepper
- 1 tablespoon chili powder

Directions:

1. In a bowl, combine cider vinegar, crushed coriander seeds, black pepper, and chili powder to create the marinade.
2. Add thinly sliced beef to the marinade and marinate for at least 2 hours or overnight.
3. Preheat the air fryer oven dehydrate function to 160°F.
4. Arrange marinated beef slices on the air fryer trays/pans and dehydrate for 4 hours or until the beef becomes biltong.

Nutritional Value (Amount per Serving):

Calories: 171; Fat: 9.86; Carb: 1.81; Protein: 17.97

Toasted Balsamic-Glazed Pork Belly

Prep Time: 20 Minutes   Cook Time: 1 Hour   Serves: 6

Ingredients:

- 2 lbs pork belly, sliced
- 1/2 cup balsamic vinegar
- 1/4 cup honey
- 2 tablespoons soy sauce
- 2 cloves garlic, minced

Directions:

1. Preheat the air fryer oven to 375°F.
2. In a small saucepan, combine balsamic vinegar, honey, soy sauce, and minced garlic. Simmer until it thickens.
3. Coat pork belly slices with the balsamic glaze and place them on the air fryer tray/pan.
4. Toast for 45-50 minutes, turning occasionally, until the pork belly is crispy and caramelized.

Nutritional Value (Amount per Serving):

Calories: 862; Fat: 81.12; Carb: 16.92; Protein: 14.71

Grilled Moroccan-Style Lamb Chops

Prep Time: 30 Minutes   Cook Time: 15 Minutes   Serves: 4

Ingredients:

- 8 lamb chops
- 2 teaspoons ground cumin
- 1 teaspoon ground coriander
- 1 teaspoon paprika
- 1 teaspoon cinnamon
- Salt and pepper to taste

Directions:

1. In a bowl, mix ground cumin, ground coriander, paprika, cinnamon, salt, and pepper.
2. Rub the spice mixture onto both sides of each lamb chop. Marinate for 20-30 minutes.
3. Preheat the air fryer oven grill function to 400°F.
4. Grill the marinated lamb chops for 8-10 minutes, turning once, until they reach your desired level of doneness.

Nutritional Value (Amount per Serving):

Calories: 334; Fat: 15.94; Carb: 2.37; Protein: 45.84

Air-Fried Asian-Style Beef Stir-Fry

Prep Time: 25 Minutes   Cook Time: 15 Minutes   Serves: 4

Ingredients:

- 1.5 lbs beef sirloin, thinly sliced
- 1 cup broccoli florets
- 1 bell pepper, sliced
- 1/2 cup soy sauce
- 2 tablespoons hoisin sauce
- 1 tablespoon sesame oil
- 2 cloves garlic, minced
- 1 teaspoon ginger, grated

Directions:

1. Preheat the air fryer oven to 400°F.
2. In a bowl, mix soy sauce, hoisin sauce, sesame oil, minced garlic, and grated ginger.
3. Place sliced beef, broccoli, and bell pepper on the air fryer pan/tray and air fry for 12-15 minutes, tossing occasionally, until beef is cooked and vegetables are tender.

Nutritional Value (Amount per Serving):

Calories: 471; Fat: 28.45; Carb: 13.39; Protein: 38.36

Roasted Garlic-Herb Pork Loin

Prep Time: 15 Minutes   Cook Time: 40 Minutes   Serves: 6

Ingredients:

- 2.5 lbs pork loin
- 4 cloves garlic, minced
- 2 tablespoons fresh thyme, chopped
- 3 tablespoons olive oil
- Salt and pepper to taste

Directions:

1. Preheat the air fryer oven roast function to 375°F.
2. Mix minced garlic, chopped thyme, olive oil, salt, and pepper.
3. Rub the pork loin with the garlic-herb mixture and place it on the roasting pan.
4. Roast in the air fryer oven for 30-35 minutes, turning once, until the internal temperature reaches 145°F.

Nutritional Value (Amount per Serving):

Calories: 461; Fat: 27.69; Carb: 1.57; Protein: 48.72

Air-Fried Chimichurri Steak Bites

Prep Time: 20 Minutes   Cook Time: 15 Minutes   Serves: 4

Ingredients:

- 1.5 lbs sirloin steak, cut into bite-sized pieces
- 1 cup fresh parsley, chopped
- 1/2 cup olive oil
- 3 tablespoons red wine vinegar
- 3 cloves garlic, minced
- Salt and pepper to taste

Directions:

1. In a blender, combine parsley, olive oil, red wine vinegar, minced garlic, salt, and pepper to make chimichurri sauce.
2. Marinate steak bites in half of the chimichurri sauce for 15 minutes.
3. Preheat the air fryer oven to 400°F.
4. Air fry the marinated steak bites for 10-12 minutes or until cooked to your liking.
5. Serve with the remaining chimichurri sauce for dipping.

Nutritional Value (Amount per Serving):

Calories: 576; Fat: 46.08; Carb: 2.79; Protein: 35.99

Dehydrated Teriyaki Beef Strips

Prep Time: 15 Minutes   Cook Time: 4 Hours   Serves: 8

Ingredients:

- 1.5 lbs flank steak, thinly sliced
- 1/2 cup teriyaki sauce
- 2 tablespoons brown sugar
- 1 teaspoon garlic powder

Directions:

1. In a bowl, mix teriyaki sauce, brown sugar, and garlic powder to create the marinade.
2. Add thinly sliced flank steak to the marinade and marinate for at least 2 hours or overnight.
3. Preheat the air fryer oven dehydrate function to 160°F.
4. Arrange marinated beef slices on the air fryer trays and dehydrate for 4 hours or until the beef becomes jerky-like.

Nutritional Value (Amount per Serving):

Calories: 137; Fat: 4.26; Carb: 3.87; Protein: 19.36

Grilled Garlic-Lemon Pork Skewers

Prep Time: 20 Minutes   Cook Time: 15 Minutes   Serves: 4

Ingredients:

- 1.5 lbs pork loin, cut into cubes
- 3 cloves garlic, minced
- Zest and juice of 1 lemon
- 2 tablespoons olive oil
- Salt and pepper to taste

Directions:

1. In a bowl, mix minced garlic, lemon zest, lemon juice, olive oil, salt, and pepper.
2. Add pork cubes to the marinade and marinate for 15 minutes.
3. Preheat the air fryer oven grill function to 400°F.
4. Thread marinated pork onto skewers and grill for 10-12 minutes, turning occasionally, until fully cooked.

Nutritional Value (Amount per Serving):

Calories: 426; Fat: 25.63; Carb: 2.64; Protein: 43.97

Baked Herb-Crusted Lamb Ribs

Prep Time: 30 Minutes   Cook Time: 1 Hour 15 Minutes   Serves: 6

Ingredients:

- 3 lbs lamb ribs
- 3 tablespoons Dijon mustard
- 1 cup panko breadcrumbs
- 2 tablespoons fresh mint, chopped
- Salt and pepper to taste

Directions:

1. Preheat the air fryer oven bake function to 375°F.
2. Brush lamb ribs with Dijon mustard, then coat with a mixture of panko breadcrumbs, chopped mint, salt, and pepper.
3. Place the ribs on the baking pan and bake for 1 hour or until the crust is crispy and the ribs are tender.

Nutritional Value (Amount per Serving):

Calories: 500; Fat: 27; Carb: 1.16; Protein: 59.16

Toasted Herb-Crusted Beef Tenderloin

Prep Time: 25 Minutes   Cook Time: 35 Minutes   Serves: 4

Ingredients:

- 1.5 lbs beef tenderloin
- 2 tablespoons Dijon mustard
- 1 cup breadcrumbs
- 2 tablespoons fresh thyme, chopped
- Salt and pepper to taste

Directions:

1. Preheat the air fryer oven to 400°F.
2. Rub beef tenderloin with Dijon mustard, then coat with a mixture of breadcrumbs, chopped thyme, salt, and pepper.
3. Place the tenderloin on the air fryer rack and toast for 30 minutes or until the crust is golden brown and the beef is cooked to your liking.

Nutritional Value (Amount per Serving):

Calories: 369; Fat: 15.46; Carb: 1.81; Protein: 52.46

Broiled Garlic-Herb Pork Chops

Prep Time: 15 Minutes   Cook Time: 20 Minutes   Serves: 5

Ingredients:

- 5 pork chops
- 3 cloves garlic, minced
- 2 tablespoons fresh rosemary, chopped
- 2 tablespoons olive oil

- Salt and pepper to taste

Directions:

1. Preheat the air fryer oven broil function to 425°F.
2. Mix minced garlic, chopped rosemary, olive oil, salt, and pepper.
3. Rub the mixture onto both sides of each pork chop.
4. Place the pork chops on the air fryer oven pan and broil for 10 minutes on each side or until the internal temperature reaches 145°F.

Nutritional Value (Amount per Serving):

Calories: 383; Fat: 22.83; Carb: 1.59; Protein: 40.52

Air-Fried BBQ Pulled Pork Sliders

Prep Time: 20 Minutes   Cook Time: 50 Minutes   Serves: 8

Ingredients:

- 2 lbs pork shoulder, shredded
- 1 cup barbecue sauce
- 8 slider buns
- 1 cup coleslaw

Directions:

1. Preheat the air fryer oven to 375°F.
2. In a bowl, mix shredded pork with barbecue sauce.
3. Place the sauced pork on the air fryer tray/pan and air fry for 30-40 minutes, stirring occasionally.
4. Assemble sliders with pulled pork and coleslaw on the buns.

Nutritional Value (Amount per Serving):

Calories: 692; Fat: 39.64; Carb: 49.9; Protein: 31.83

Chapter 4: Fish and Seafood

Lemon Garlic Grilled Shrimp Skewers

Prep Time: 15 Minutes   Cook Time: 10 Minutes   Serves: 4

Ingredients:

- 1 pound large shrimp, peeled and deveined
- 2 tablespoons olive oil
- 3 cloves garlic, minced
- 1 lemon, juiced
- 1 teaspoon dried oregano
- Salt and pepper to taste
- Wooden skewers, soaked in water

Directions:

1. In a bowl, mix olive oil, minced garlic, lemon juice, oregano, salt, and pepper to create a marinade.
2. Thread shrimp onto the soaked skewers and coat with the marinade.
3. Preheat the Grill function of the Air Fryer Oven at 400°F.
4. Grill shrimp skewers for 3-4 minutes per side until they are opaque and lightly charred.
5. Serve immediately with your favorite side dishes.

Nutritional Value (Amount per Serving):

Calories: 84; Fat: 7; Carb: 5.26; Protein: 1.1

Crispy Baked Cod with Herbed Parmesan Crust

Prep Time: 20 Minutes   Cook Time: 15 Minutes   Serves: 4

Ingredients:

- 4 cod fillets
- 1 cup breadcrumbs
- 1/2 cup grated Parmesan cheese
- 2 tablespoons chopped fresh parsley
- 1 teaspoon dried thyme
- Salt and pepper to taste
- Olive oil spray

Directions:

1. Preheat the Bake function of the Air Fryer Oven to 375°F.
2. In a bowl, combine breadcrumbs, Parmesan, parsley, thyme, salt, and pepper.
3. Coat each cod fillet with the breadcrumb mixture, pressing gently to adhere.

4. Place fillets on the air fryer tray and lightly spray with olive oil.
5. Bake for 12-15 minutes or until the crust is golden and the fish flakes easily with a fork.

Nutritional Value (Amount per Serving):

Calories: 201; Fat: 11.1; Carb: 2.97; Protein: 21.56

Cajun Spiced Air-Fried Catfish

Prep Time: 15 Minutes   Cook Time: 12 Minutes   Serves: 4

Ingredients:

- 4 catfish fillets
- 2 tablespoons Cajun seasoning
- 1 tablespoon olive oil
- 1 teaspoon paprika
- 1/2 teaspoon garlic powder
- 1/2 teaspoon onion powder
- Lemon wedges for serving

Directions:

1. Preheat the Air Fry function of the Air Fryer Oven to 375°F.
2. Rub catfish fillets with Cajun seasoning, olive oil, paprika, garlic powder, and onion powder.
3. Place fillets on the air fryer tray, ensuring they are not crowded.
4. Air fry for 10-12 minutes, flipping halfway, until the fish is crispy and cooked through.
5. Serve with lemon wedges.

Nutritional Value (Amount per Serving):

Calories: 201; Fat: 7.97; Carb: 4.15; Protein: 26.46

Teriyaki Glazed Salmon with Pineapple

Prep Time: 25 Minutes   Cook Time: 18 Minutes   Serves: 4

Ingredients:

- 4 salmon fillets
- 1/2 cup teriyaki sauce
- 2 tablespoons honey
- 1 tablespoon soy sauce
- 1 teaspoon grated ginger
- 1 cup fresh pineapple chunks

Directions:

1. Preheat the Roast function of the Air Fryer Oven to 400°F.
2. In a bowl, mix teriyaki sauce, honey, soy sauce, and grated ginger.
3. Place salmon fillets on the air fryer trays, surround with pineapple chunks, and pour the teriyaki mixture over them.
4. Roast for 15-18 minutes or until salmon is cooked through, basting with

the sauce halfway.

Nutritional Value (Amount per Serving):

Calories: 215; Fat: 4.86; Carb: 28.94; Protein: 14.4

Mediterranean Style Grilled Swordfish

Prep Time: 30 Minutes   Cook Time: 14 Minutes   Serves: 4

Ingredients:

- 4 swordfish steaks
- 1/4 cup olive oil
- 2 tablespoons lemon juice
- 3 cloves garlic, minced
- 1 teaspoon dried oregano
- Salt and pepper to taste
- Cherry tomatoes and olives for garnish

Directions:

1. Preheat the Grill function of the Air Fryer Oven to 400°F.
2. In a bowl, whisk together olive oil, lemon juice, minced garlic, oregano, salt, and pepper.
3. Brush swordfish steaks with the marinade and let them marinate for 15-20 minutes.
4. Grill the swordfish for 6-7 minutes per side until they are cooked through and have grill marks.
5. Garnish with cherry tomatoes and olives before serving.

Nutritional Value (Amount per Serving):

Calories: 625; Fat: 46.29; Carb: 2.83; Protein: 46.82

Herb-Crusted Air-Fried Halibut

Prep Time: 20 Minutes   Cook Time: 15 Minutes   Serves: 4

Ingredients:

- 4 halibut fillets
- 1 cup breadcrumbs
- 2 tablespoons chopped fresh herbs (parsley, dill, and chives)
- 1 teaspoon garlic powder
- Salt and pepper to taste
- 2 tablespoons olive oil

Directions:

1. Preheat the Air Fry function of the Air Fryer Oven to 400°F.
2. In a bowl, mix breadcrumbs, chopped herbs, garlic powder, salt, and pepper.

3. Coat halibut fillets with olive oil and dredge in the breadcrumb mixture.
4. Air fry for 12-15 minutes until the crust is golden and the fish is cooked through.

Nutritional Value (Amount per Serving):

Calories: 826; Fat: 63.26; Carb: 1.26; Protein: 59.03

Crispy Breaded Coconut Shrimp

Prep Time: 30 Minutes   Cook Time: 12 Minutes   Serves: 4

Ingredients:

- 1 pound large shrimp, peeled and deveined
- 1 cup shredded coconut
- 1 cup breadcrumbs
- 2 eggs, beaten
- Salt and pepper to taste
- Sweet chili sauce for dipping

Directions:

1. Preheat the Air Fry function of the Air Fryer Oven to 375°F.
2. In separate bowls, place shredded coconut and breadcrumbs.
3. Dip shrimp in beaten eggs, then coat with shredded coconut and breadcrumbs mixture.
4. Air fry for 10-12 minutes until shrimp are golden and crispy.
5. Serve with sweet chili sauce.

Nutritional Value (Amount per Serving):

Calories: 102; Fat: 5.16; Carb: 7.65; Protein: 5.99

Pesto and Sundried Tomato Stuffed Calamari

Prep Time: 25 Minutes   Cook Time: 18 Minutes   Serves: 4

Ingredients:

- 8 small calamari tubes, cleaned
- 1/2 cup pesto sauce
- 1/4 cup chopped sundried tomatoes
- 2 tablespoons olive oil
- Salt and pepper to taste
- Toothpicks

Directions:

1. Preheat the Bake function of the Air Fryer Oven to 375°F.

2. In a bowl, mix pesto sauce and chopped sundried tomatoes.
3. Stuff each calamari tube with the pesto mixture and secure with toothpicks.
4. Place stuffed calamari on the baking tray, drizzle with olive oil, and season with salt and pepper.
5. Bake for 15-18 minutes until calamari is cooked and lightly browned.

Nutritional Value (Amount per Serving):

Calories: 613; Fat: 58.07; Carb: 5.24; Protein: 19.24

Honey Soy Glazed Air-Fried Tuna Steaks

Prep Time: 20 Minutes   Cook Time: 12 Minutes   Serves: 4

Ingredients:

- 4 tuna steaks
- 1/4 cup soy sauce
- 2 tablespoons honey
- 1 tablespoon sesame oil
- 1 teaspoon grated ginger
- 2 cloves garlic, minced

Directions:

1. Preheat the Air Fry function of the Air Fryer Oven to 400°F.
2. In a bowl, whisk together soy sauce, honey, sesame oil, grated ginger, and minced garlic.
3. Brush tuna steaks with the soy glaze.
4. Air fry for 5-6 minutes per side until tuna is seared and glazed.
5. Serve immediately.

Nutritional Value (Amount per Serving):

Calories: 605; Fat: 39.02; Carb: 13.2; Protein: 47.65

Garlic Butter Lobster Tails

Prep Time: 15 Minutes   Cook Time: 12 Minutes   Serves: 4

Ingredients:

- 4 lobster tails, split
- 1/2 cup melted butter
- 4 cloves garlic, minced
- 1 tablespoon chopped fresh parsley
- Salt and pepper to taste
- Lemon wedges for serving

Directions:

1. Preheat the Roast function of the Air Fryer Oven to 400°F.
2. Place lobster tails on the roasting pan.
3. In a bowl, mix melted butter, minced garlic, parsley, salt, and pepper.
4. Brush lobster tails with the garlic butter mixture.
5. Roast for 10-12 minutes or until lobster meat is opaque.
6. Serve with lemon wedges.

Nutritional Value (Amount per Serving):

Calories: 296; Fat: 24.13; Carb: 16.38; Protein: 5.09

Blackened Red Snapper

Prep Time: 20 Minutes   Cook Time: 10 Minutes   Serves: 4

Ingredients:

- 4 red snapper fillets
- 2 tablespoons Cajun seasoning
- 2 tablespoons olive oil
- 1 teaspoon smoked paprika
- 1/2 teaspoon dried thyme
- 1/2 teaspoon onion powder

Directions:

1. Preheat the Grill function of the Air Fryer Oven to 400°F.
2. Rub snapper fillets with Cajun seasoning, olive oil, smoked paprika, thyme, and onion powder.
3. Grill for 4-5 minutes per side until the fish is blackened and cooked through.
4. Serve immediately.

Nutritional Value (Amount per Serving):

Calories: 128; Fat: 6.9; Carb: 16.3; Protein: 0.78

Citrus-Marinated Swordfish Kebabs

Prep Time: 25 Minutes   Cook Time: 15 Minutes   Serves: 4

Ingredients:

- 1.5 pounds swordfish, cut into chunks
- 1 orange, juiced
- 1 lemon, juiced
- 2 tablespoons olive oil

- 2 cloves garlic, minced
- 1 teaspoon dried oregano
- Cherry tomatoes and bell pepper chunks for skewering

Directions:

1. Preheat the Grill function of the Air Fryer Oven to 400°F.
2. In a bowl, mix orange juice, lemon juice, olive oil, minced garlic, and oregano.
3. Marinate swordfish chunks in the citrus mixture for 15 minutes.
4. Thread swordfish, cherry tomatoes, and bell pepper onto skewers.
5. Grill for 6-8 minutes, turning occasionally until fish is cooked and vegetables are tender.

Nutritional Value (Amount per Serving):

Calories: 342; Fat: 18.19; Carb: 9.01; Protein: 34.05

Coconut-Curry Air-Fried Scallops

Prep Time: 20 Minutes   Cook Time: 8 Minutes   Serves: 4

Ingredients:

- 1 pound sea scallops
- 1/2 cup coconut milk
- 2 tablespoons red curry paste
- 1 tablespoon lime juice
- 1 teaspoon fish sauce
- Fresh cilantro for garnish

Directions:

1. Preheat the Air Fry function of the Air Fryer Oven to 375°F.
2. In a bowl, whisk together coconut milk, red curry paste, lime juice, and fish sauce.
3. Dip scallops in the coconut curry mixture.
4. Air fry for 4 minutes per side until scallops are opaque and lightly browned.
5. Garnish with fresh cilantro.

Nutritional Value (Amount per Serving):

Calories: 208; Fat: 8.59; Carb: 10.19; Protein: 24.67

Teriyaki Pineapple Salmon Skewers

Prep Time: 25 Minutes   Cook Time: 12 Minutes   Serves: 4

Ingredients:

- 1.5 pounds salmon, cut into chunks
- 1/2 cup teriyaki sauce
- 1/4 cup pineapple juice
- 2 tablespoons brown sugar
- Pineapple chunks for skewering

Directions:

1. Preheat the Grill function of the Air Fryer Oven to 400°F.
2. In a bowl, mix teriyaki sauce, pineapple juice, and brown sugar.
3. Marinate salmon chunks in the teriyaki mixture for 15 minutes.
4. Thread salmon and pineapple onto skewers.
5. Grill for 6-8 minutes, turning occasionally until salmon is cooked through.

Nutritional Value (Amount per Serving):

Calories: 345; Fat: 12.27; Carb: 19.4; Protein: 37.56

Lemon Herb Baked Trout

Prep Time: 20 Minutes   Cook Time: 15 Minutes   Serves: 4

Ingredients:

- 4 whole trout, gutted and cleaned
- 1 lemon, sliced
- 2 tablespoons chopped fresh dill
- 2 tablespoons chopped fresh parsley
- 3 tablespoons olive oil
- Salt and pepper to taste

Directions:

1. Preheat the Bake function of the Air Fryer Oven to 375°F.
2. Make diagonal cuts on both sides of the trout.
3. Stuff trout with lemon slices, dill, and parsley.
4. Drizzle trout with olive oil, and season with salt and pepper.
5. Bake for 12-15 minutes or until the fish flakes easily.

Nutritional Value (Amount per Serving):

Calories: 246; Fat: 18.04; Carb: 14.72; Protein: 7.99

Grilled Tandoori Shrimp Skewers

Prep Time: 25 Minutes   Cook Time: 10 Minutes   Serves: 4

Ingredients:

- 1 pound large shrimp, peeled and deveined
- 1/2 cup plain yogurt
- 2 tablespoons tandoori spice blend
- 1 tablespoon lemon juice
- 1 teaspoon minced ginger
- Fresh cilantro for garnish

Directions:

1. Preheat the Grill function of the Air Fryer Oven to 400°F.
2. In a bowl, mix yogurt, tandoori spice blend, lemon juice, and minced ginger.
3. Coat shrimp with the tandoori marinade.
4. Thread shrimp onto skewers.
5. Grill for 4-5 minutes per side until shrimp are opaque.
6. Garnish with fresh cilantro.

Nutritional Value (Amount per Serving):

Calories: 45; Fat: 1.58; Carb: 6.43; Protein: 2.07

Mediterranean Stuffed Squid

Prep Time: 30 Minutes   Cook Time: 18 Minutes   Serves: 4

Ingredients:

- 8 small squid tubes, cleaned
- 1/2 cup cooked quinoa
- 1/4 cup crumbled feta cheese
- 2 tablespoons chopped Kalamata olives
- 1 tablespoon chopped fresh parsley
- 2 tablespoons olive oil
- Salt and pepper to taste

Directions:

1. Preheat the Bake function of the Air Fryer Oven to 375°F.
2. In a bowl, mix cooked quinoa, feta cheese, Kalamata olives, parsley, olive oil, salt, and pepper.
3. Stuff squid tubes with the quinoa mixture.
4. Place stuffed squid on the baking tray.
5. Bake for 15-18 minutes or until squid is cooked through.

Nutritional Value (Amount per Serving):

Calories: 226; Fat: 11.23; Carb: 10.19; Protein: 20.13

Panko-Crusted Air-Fried Oysters

Prep Time: 20 Minutes   Cook Time: 8 Minutes   Serves: 4

Ingredients:

- 1 dozen fresh oysters, shucked
- 1 cup panko breadcrumbs
- 1/2 cup flour
- 2 eggs, beaten
- Salt and pepper to taste
- Lemon wedges for serving

Directions:

1. Preheat the Air Fry function of the Air Fryer Oven to 375°F.
2. Dredge each shucked oyster in flour, dip in beaten eggs, and coat with panko breadcrumbs.
3. Place breaded oysters in the air fryer tray, ensuring they are not crowded.
4. Air fry for 6-8 minutes until the oysters are golden and crispy.
5. Serve with lemon wedges.

Nutritional Value (Amount per Serving):

Calories: 130; Fat: 5.07; Carb: 14.4; Protein: 6.51

Mediterranean Stuffed Mussels

Prep Time: 25 Minutes   Cook Time: 15 Minutes   Serves: 4

Ingredients:

- 2 pounds fresh mussels, cleaned and debearded
- 1/2 cup breadcrumbs
- 1/4 cup grated Parmesan cheese
- 2 tablespoons chopped fresh parsley
- 1/4 cup finely diced tomatoes
- 2 tablespoons olive oil
- 2 cloves garlic, minced
- 1/4 cup white wine
- Salt and pepper to taste
- Lemon wedges for serving

Directions:

1. Preheat the Air Fry function of the Air Fryer Oven to 375°F.
2. In a bowl, mix breadcrumbs, Parmesan cheese, chopped parsley, diced tomatoes, olive oil, minced garlic, salt, and pepper.
3. Clean and debeard the mussels, discarding any that are open or broken.

4. Fill each mussel with the breadcrumb mixture.
5. Place the stuffed mussels on the air fryer tray/pan, ensuring they are not overcrowded.
6. Drizzle white wine over the mussels.
7. Air fry for 12-15 minutes until the mussels open, and the stuffing is golden brown and cooked through.
8. Serve with lemon wedges.

Nutritional Value (Amount per Serving):

Calories: 294; Fat: 13.66; Carb: 12.27; Protein: 29.34

Crispy Coconut-Curry Air-Fried Shrimp

Prep Time: 20 Minutes   Cook Time: 10 Minutes   Serves: 4

Ingredients:

- 1 pound large shrimp, peeled and deveined
- 1 cup shredded coconut
- 1/2 cup panko breadcrumbs
- 2 eggs, beaten
- 1/4 cup coconut milk
- 2 tablespoons red curry paste
- Salt and pepper to taste
- Sweet chili sauce for dipping

Directions:

1. Preheat the Air Fry function of the Air Fryer Oven to 375°F.
2. In separate bowls, place shredded coconut and panko breadcrumbs.
3. In another bowl, mix beaten eggs, coconut milk, and red curry paste.
4. Dip each shrimp in the egg mixture, then coat with a mixture of shredded coconut and panko breadcrumbs.
5. Place the coated shrimp on the air fryer tray/pan, ensuring they are not crowded.
6. Air fry for 6-8 minutes until the shrimp are golden and crispy.
7. Serve with sweet chili sauce for dipping.

Nutritional Value (Amount per Serving):

Calories: 146; Fat: 9.18; Carb: 10.24; Protein: 6.78

Chapter 5: Vegetables and Sides

Dehydrated Sweet Potato Chips

Prep Time: 15 Minutes   Cook Time: 6 Hours   Serves: 4-6

Ingredients:

- 2 large sweet potatoes, peeled
- 2 tablespoons olive oil
- 1 teaspoon smoked paprika
- 1/2 teaspoon sea salt
- 1/4 teaspoon black pepper

Directions:

1. Preheat the Dehydrate function of the Air Fryer Oven to 135°F.
2. Using a mandoline slicer or a sharp knife, thinly slice sweet potatoes into rounds.
3. In a large bowl, toss sweet potato slices with olive oil, smoked paprika, sea salt, and black pepper until evenly coated.
4. Arrange the sweet potato slices on the air fryer trays in a single layer, ensuring they are not touching.
5. Dehydrate for 6 hours or until the sweet potato chips are crisp. Rotate the trays halfway through for even dehydration.
6. Allow the chips to cool completely before serving. They will continue to crisp up as they cool.

Nutritional Value (Amount per Serving):

Calories: 114; Fat: 5.57; Carb: 15.25; Protein: 1.53

Roasted Garlic Parmesan Brussels Sprouts

Prep Time: 10 Minutes   Cook Time: 25 Minutes   Serves: 4-6

Ingredients:

- 1 lb Brussels sprouts, trimmed and halved
- 3 tablespoons olive oil
- 4 cloves garlic, minced
- 1/2 cup grated Parmesan cheese
- Salt and pepper to taste

Directions:

1. Preheat the Air Fryer Oven to 375°F.
2. In a large bowl, toss Brussels sprouts with olive oil, minced garlic, Parmesan cheese, salt, and pepper until well coated.
3. Place the Brussels sprouts in a single layer on the air fryer trays.
4. Air fry for 20-25 minutes, shaking the trays halfway through, until the Brussels sprouts are golden and crispy.
5. Serve hot and enjoy the crispy, flavorful goodness.

Nutritional Value (Amount per Serving):

Calories: 160; Fat: 11.19; Carb: 11.16; Protein: 6.24

Herb-Roasted Sweet Potatoes and Carrots

Prep Time: 15 Minutes   Cook Time: 30 Minutes   Serves: 4-6

Ingredients:

- 2 sweet potatoes, peeled and cubed
- 4 carrots, peeled and sliced
- 3 tablespoons olive oil
- 1 teaspoon dried thyme
- 1 teaspoon dried rosemary
- Salt and pepper to taste

Directions:

1. Preheat the Air Fryer Oven to 400°F.
2. In a large bowl, toss sweet potatoes and carrots with olive oil, dried thyme, dried rosemary, salt, and pepper.
3. Spread the vegetables evenly on the air fryer trays.
4. Roast for 25-30 minutes until the edges are golden brown, tossing once halfway through.
5. Serve as a colorful and flavorful side dish.

Nutritional Value (Amount per Serving):

Calories: 91; Fat: 8.31; Carb: 4.15; Protein: 1.06

Dehydrated Zucchini Chips

Prep Time: 10 Minutes   Cook Time: 4 Hours   Serves: 4-6

Ingredients:

- 4 medium zucchinis, thinly sliced
- 2 tablespoons olive oil
- 1 teaspoon garlic powder
- 1 teaspoon onion powder
- 1/2 teaspoon paprika
- Salt to taste

Directions:

1. Preheat the Dehydrate function of the Air Fryer Oven to 135°F.
2. In a bowl, toss zucchini slices with olive oil, garlic powder, onion powder, paprika, and salt.
3. Arrange zucchini slices on the air fryer trays in a single layer.
4. Dehydrate for 4 hours or until the zucchini chips are crispy.
5. Allow to cool before serving.

Nutritional Value (Amount per Serving):

Calories: 54; Fat: 5.48; Carb: 1.23; Protein: 0.42

Grilled Lemon Garlic Asparagus

Prep Time: 5 Minutes   Cook Time: 15 Minutes   Serves: 4-6

Ingredients:

- 1 lb fresh asparagus, trimmed
- 2 tablespoons olive oil
- 2 cloves garlic, minced
- Zest of 1 lemon
- Salt and pepper to taste

Directions:

1. Preheat the Grill function of the Air Fryer Oven to 375°F.
2. In a bowl, toss asparagus with olive oil, minced garlic, lemon zest, salt, and pepper.
3. Place asparagus directly on the grill grate.
4. Grill for 12-15 minutes, turning occasionally, until asparagus is tender and slightly charred.
5. Serve with a squeeze of fresh lemon juice.

Nutritional Value (Amount per Serving):

Calories: 73; Fat: 5.56; Carb: 5.43; Protein: 2.29

Crispy Parmesan Zucchini Chips

Prep Time: 15 Minutes   Cook Time: 20 Minutes   Serves: 4-6

Ingredients:

- 4 medium-sized zucchinis, thinly sliced
- 1 cup breadcrumbs
- 1 cup grated Parmesan cheese
- 2 teaspoons garlic powder
- Salt and pepper to taste
- Olive oil spray

Directions:

1. Preheat the Air Fryer Oven to 375°F.
2. In a bowl, combine breadcrumbs, Parmesan cheese, garlic powder, salt, and pepper.
3. Dip each zucchini slice into the breadcrumb mixture, ensuring even coating.
4. Place the coated zucchini slices on a single layer in the Air Fryer tray/pan.
5. Lightly spray the slices with olive oil.
6. Air fry for 10 minutes, flip the slices, and air fry for an additional 10 minutes or until golden and crispy.
7. Serve immediately and enjoy the crunchy goodness.

Nutritional Value (Amount per Serving):

Calories: 144; Fat: 11.31; Carb: 4.81; Protein: 6.31

Sweet Potato Wedges with Cinnamon Sugar

Prep Time: 15 Minutes   Cook Time: 30 Minutes   Serves: 4-6

Ingredients:

- 3 large sweet potatoes, cut into wedges
- 2 tablespoons olive oil
- 1 teaspoon ground cinnamon
- 2 tablespoons brown sugar
- Pinch of salt

Directions:

1. Preheat the Air Fryer Oven to 375°F.
2. In a bowl, toss sweet potato wedges with olive oil, cinnamon, brown sugar, and a pinch of salt.
3. Arrange the wedges on a single layer in the Air Fryer tray/pan.
4. Air fry for 15 minutes, flip the wedges, and air fry for an additional 15 minutes or until they are crispy on the outside and tender on the inside.
5. Serve warm, and enjoy the delightful sweetness.

Nutritional Value (Amount per Serving):

Calories: 151; Fat: 5.57; Carb: 24.04; Protein: 2.19

Stuffed Bell Peppers with Quinoa and Black Beans

Prep Time: 20 Minutes   Cook Time: 35 Minutes   Serves: 4-6

Ingredients:

- 4 large bell peppers, halved and cleaned
- 1 cup cooked quinoa
- 1 can black beans, drained and rinsed
- 1 cup corn kernels
- 1 cup diced tomatoes
- 1 cup shredded cheddar cheese
- 1 teaspoon ground cumin
- Salt and pepper to taste

Directions:

1. Preheat the Bake function of the Air Fryer Oven to 375°F.
2. In a bowl, mix quinoa, black beans, corn, tomatoes, cheddar cheese,

ground cumin, salt, and pepper.
3. Stuff each bell pepper half with the quinoa mixture.
4. Arrange the stuffed peppers on the baking rack.
5. Bake for 20-25 minutes or until the peppers are tender, and the filling is heated through.

Nutritional Value (Amount per Serving):

Calories: 265; Fat: 4.56; Carb: 43.15; Protein: 15.69

Roasted Cauliflower Steaks with Chimichurri Sauce

Prep Time: 15 Minutes   Cook Time: 25 Minutes   Serves: 4-6

Ingredients:

- 2 large cauliflower heads, sliced into steaks
- 3 tablespoons olive oil
- 1 teaspoon smoked paprika
- Salt and pepper to taste
- 1 cup fresh parsley, chopped
- 1/4 cup fresh cilantro, chopped
- 3 cloves garlic, minced
- 1/2 cup olive oil
- 2 tablespoons red wine vinegar
- Salt and pepper to taste

Directions:

1. Preheat the Roast function of the Air Fryer Oven to 400°F.
2. In a bowl, toss cauliflower steaks with olive oil, smoked paprika, salt, and pepper.
3. Place the cauliflower steaks on the air fryer oven pan.
4. Roast for 20-25 minutes or until golden and tender, flipping halfway through.
5. While cauliflower is roasting, prepare the chimichurri sauce by mixing all sauce ingredients in a bowl.
6. Drizzle the chimichurri sauce over the roasted cauliflower steaks before serving.

Nutritional Value (Amount per Serving):

Calories: 306; Fat: 30.2; Carb: 8.62; Protein: 2.95

Sweet and Spicy Roasted Butternut Squash

Prep Time: 15 Minutes   Cook Time: 30 Minutes   Serves: 4-6

- 1 medium butternut squash, peeled and diced
- 2 tablespoons olive oil
- 2 tablespoons honey
- 1 teaspoon chili powder
- 1/2 teaspoon cinnamon
- Salt and pepper to taste

Directions:

1. Preheat the Roast function of the Air Fryer Oven to 375°F.
2. In a bowl, toss diced butternut squash with olive oil, honey, chili powder, cinnamon, salt, and pepper.
3. Spread the seasoned butternut squash on the air fryer pan.
4. Roast for 25-30 minutes or until the squash is caramelized and fork-tender, stirring halfway through.

Nutritional Value (Amount per Serving):

Calories: 169; Fat: 5.7; Carb: 31.63; Protein: 2.29

Hasselback Sweet Potatoes with Maple Pecan Glaze

Prep Time: 20 Minutes   Cook Time: 40 Minutes   Serves: 4-6

Ingredients:

- 4 medium sweet potatoes, scrubbed
- 1/4 cup melted butter
- 2 tablespoons maple syrup
- 1/2 cup chopped pecans
- 1 teaspoon cinnamon
- Salt to taste

Directions:

1. Preheat the Bake function of the Air Fryer Oven to 400°F.
2. Cut thin slices along each sweet potato, being careful not to cut through.
3. In a bowl, mix melted butter, maple syrup, chopped pecans, cinnamon, and a pinch of salt.
4. Brush the sweet potatoes with the maple pecan glaze, ensuring it gets between the slices.
5. Place the sweet potatoes in the baking pan.
6. Bake for 35-40 minutes or until the sweet potatoes are tender and the edges are crispy.

Nutritional Value (Amount per Serving):

Calories: 264; Fat: 16.52; Carb: 28.57; Protein: 2.68

Lemon Butter Roasted Cabbage Steaks

Prep Time: 15 Minutes   Cook Time: 25 Minutes   Serves: 4-6

Ingredients:

- 1 head cabbage, sliced into steaks
- 1/4 cup melted butter
- Juice of 1 lemon
- 2 teaspoons Dijon mustard
- 2 cloves garlic, minced
- Salt and pepper to taste

Directions:

1. Preheat the Roast function of the Air Fryer Oven to 375°F.
2. In a bowl, whisk together melted butter, lemon juice, Dijon mustard, minced garlic, salt, and pepper.
3. Brush the cabbage steaks with the lemon butter mixture.
4. Place the cabbage steaks on the roasting pan.
5. Roast for 20-25 minutes or until the edges are golden and the cabbage is tender.

Nutritional Value (Amount per Serving):

Calories: 125; Fat: 9.51; Carb: 10.39; Protein: 2.08

Caramelized Onion and Gruyère Tart

Prep Time: 20 Minutes   Cook Time: 25 Minutes   Serves: 4-6

Ingredients:

- 1 sheet puff pastry, thawed
- 2 large onions, thinly sliced
- 2 tablespoons olive oil
- 1 teaspoon balsamic vinegar
- 1 cup Gruyère cheese, shredded
- Fresh thyme leaves (for garnish)

Directions:

1. Preheat the Bake function of the Air Fryer Oven to 375°F.
2. In a pan, sauté onions with olive oil and balsamic vinegar until caramelized.
3. Roll out the puff pastry and place it in the baking pan.
4. Spread the caramelized onions over the pastry and sprinkle with Gruyère cheese.
5. Bake for 20-25 minutes or until the pastry is golden and the cheese is melted.
6. Garnish with fresh thyme leaves before serving.

Nutritional Value (Amount per Serving):

Calories: 276; Fat: 20.01; Carb: 18.13; Protein: 7.05

Southwest Cornbread Casserole

Prep Time: 20 Minutes   Cook Time: 25 Minutes   Serves: 4-6

Ingredients:

- 1 box cornbread mix
- 1/2 cup milk
- 1/4 cup melted butter
- 1 can (15 oz) black beans, drained and rinsed
- 1 cup corn kernels
- 1 cup diced bell peppers
- 1 cup shredded cheddar cheese
- 1 teaspoon ground cumin
- 1 teaspoon chili powder
- Salt and pepper to taste

Directions:

1. Preheat the Bake function of the Air Fryer Oven to 375°F.
2. In a bowl, prepare the cornbread mix according to package instructions, adding milk and melted butter.
3. In another bowl, mix black beans, corn, bell peppers, cheddar cheese, ground cumin, chili powder, salt, and pepper.
4. Spread the cornbread batter in the baking pan and top with the black bean mixture.
5. Bake for 20-25 minutes or until the cornbread is golden and cooked through.

Nutritional Value (Amount per Serving):

Calories: 846; Fat: 62.73; Carb: 50.75; Protein: 31.87

Teriyaki Glazed Grilled Eggplant

Prep Time: 15 Minutes   Cook Time: 20 Minutes   Serves: 4-6

Ingredients:

- 2 large eggplants, sliced
- 1/2 cup teriyaki sauce
- 2 tablespoons sesame oil
- 1 tablespoon sesame seeds
- Green onions, sliced (for garnish)

Directions:

1. Preheat the Grill function of the Air Fryer Oven to 375°F.
2. In a bowl, mix eggplant slices with teriyaki sauce and sesame oil.

3. Grill the eggplant slices for 10 minutes, turning halfway through.
4. Sprinkle sesame seeds and green onions on top before serving.

Nutritional Value (Amount per Serving):

Calories: 140; Fat: 6.85; Carb: 17.89; Protein: 4.24

Caprese Stuffed Portobello Mushrooms

Prep Time: 15 Minutes   Cook Time: 20 Minutes   Serves: 4

Ingredients:

- 4 large Portobello mushrooms, cleaned and stemmed
- 1 cup cherry tomatoes, halved
- 1 cup fresh mozzarella, diced
- 1/4 cup fresh basil, chopped
- 2 tablespoons balsamic glaze
- Salt and pepper to taste

Directions:

1. Preheat the Bake function of the Air Fryer Oven to 375°F.
2. In a bowl, mix cherry tomatoes, mozzarella, basil, balsamic glaze, salt, and pepper.
3. Stuff each mushroom with the tomato and mozzarella mixture.
4. Place the stuffed mushrooms in the baking pan.
5. Bake for 15-20 minutes or until the mushrooms are tender and the cheese is melted.

Nutritional Value (Amount per Serving):

Calories: 73; Fat: 0.47; Carb: 7.23; Protein: 11.73

Roasted Rainbow Carrots with Dill Yogurt Sauce

Prep Time: 15 Minutes   Cook Time: 25 Minutes   Serves: 4-6

Ingredients:

- 1 pound rainbow carrots, peeled and trimmed
- 2 tablespoons olive oil
- 1 teaspoon ground cumin
- Salt and pepper to taste
- 1 cup Greek yogurt
- 2 tablespoons fresh dill, chopped
- 1 tablespoon lemon juice
- Salt and pepper to taste

Directions:

1. Preheat the Roast function of the Air Fryer Oven to 400°F.

2. In a bowl, toss rainbow carrots with olive oil, ground cumin, salt, and pepper.
3. Place the carrots on the roasting pan.
4. Roast for 20-25 minutes or until the carrots are golden and tender.
5. Meanwhile, mix Greek yogurt, chopped dill, lemon juice, salt, and pepper for the sauce.
6. Serve the roasted carrots with a side of dill yogurt sauce.

Nutritional Value (Amount per Serving):

Calories: 107; Fat: 6.15; Carb: 11.63; Protein: 3.29

Smoky Maple Roasted Acorn Squash

Prep Time: 15 Minutes   Cook Time: 30 Minutes   Serves: 4-6

Ingredients:

- 2 acorn squash, halved and seeds removed
- 1/4 cup melted butter
- 2 tablespoons maple syrup
- 1 teaspoon smoked paprika
- 1/2 teaspoon ground cinnamon
- Salt and pepper to taste
- Pomegranate arils (for garnish)

Directions:

1. Preheat the Roast function of the Air Fryer Oven to 375°F.
2. In a bowl, mix melted butter, maple syrup, smoked paprika, ground cinnamon, salt, and pepper.
3. Brush the cut sides of acorn squash with the maple butter mixture.
4. Place the acorn squash halves in the roasting pan.
5. Roast for 25-30 minutes or until the squash is tender.
6. Garnish with pomegranate arils before serving.

Nutritional Value (Amount per Serving):

Calories: 224; Fat: 10.13; Carb: 35.19; Protein: 2.68

Crispy Chickpea and Spinach Stuffed Mushrooms

Prep Time: 20 Minutes   Cook Time: 25 Minutes   Serves: 4-6

Ingredients:

- 12 large mushrooms, cleaned and stemmed
- 1 can (15 oz) chickpeas, drained and rinsed
- 2 cups baby spinach, chopped

- 1/2 cup feta cheese, crumbled
- 2 tablespoons olive oil
- 1 teaspoon smoked paprika
- Salt and pepper to taste

Directions:

1. Preheat the Roast function of the Air Fryer Oven to 375°F.
2. In a food processor, pulse chickpeas until coarsely chopped.
3. In a pan, sauté chopped spinach with olive oil until wilted.
4. In a bowl, mix chopped chickpeas, sautéed spinach, feta cheese, smoked paprika, salt, and pepper.
5. Stuff each mushroom with the chickpea and spinach mixture.
6. Place the stuffed mushrooms in the roasting pan.
7. Roast for 20-25 minutes or until the mushrooms are tender and filling is crispy.

Nutritional Value (Amount per Serving):

Calories: 193; Fat: 10.47; Carb: 17.76; Protein: 9.92

Spicy Roasted Brussels Sprouts with Sriracha Honey Glaze

Prep Time: 15 Minutes   Cook Time: 25 Minutes   Serves: 4-6

Ingredients:

- 1 pound Brussels sprouts, trimmed and halved
- 2 tablespoons olive oil
- 2 tablespoons soy sauce
- 1 tablespoon Sriracha sauce
- 2 tablespoons honey
- 1 teaspoon garlic powder
- Sesame seeds (for garnish)

Directions:

1. Preheat the Roast function of the Air Fryer Oven to 400°F.
2. In a bowl, toss Brussels sprouts with olive oil, soy sauce, Sriracha sauce, honey, and garlic powder.
3. Spread the Brussels sprouts on the roasting pan.
4. Roast for 20-25 minutes, shaking the pan halfway through, until sprouts are crispy.
5. Garnish with sesame seeds before serving.

Nutritional Value (Amount per Serving):

Calories: 170; Fat: 10.31; Carb: 17.99; Protein: 4.87

Chapter 6: Breads and Pizzas

Garlic Herb Focaccia Bread

Prep Time: 15 Minutes   Cook Time: 25 Minutes   Serves: 6

Ingredients:

- 2 1/2 cups all-purpose flour
- 1 tablespoon sugar
- 1 tablespoon active dry yeast
- 1 cup warm water
- 3 tablespoons olive oil
- 2 cloves garlic, minced
- 1 teaspoon dried rosemary
- Salt and pepper to taste

Directions:

1. In a bowl, combine warm water, sugar, and yeast. Let it sit for 5 minutes until foamy.
2. In a large mixing bowl, combine flour, olive oil, minced garlic, rosemary, salt, and pepper. Add the yeast mixture and knead until a soft dough forms.
3. Divide the dough in half and roll each portion into a rectangular shape. Place them on the baking trays of the French Door Air Fryer Oven.
4. Set the oven to the Bake function at 375°F for 20 minutes, or until golden brown.
5. Remove from the oven, slice, and serve warm.

Nutritional Value (Amount per Serving):

Calories: 266; Fat: 7.44; Carb: 42.96; Protein: 6.41

Margherita Pizza with Crispy Crust

Prep Time: 20 Minutes   Cook Time: 15 Minutes   Serves: 4

Ingredients:

- 1 pound pizza dough
- 1/2 cup pizza sauce
- 1 1/2 cups fresh mozzarella, sliced
- 2 medium tomatoes, thinly sliced
- Fresh basil leaves
- Olive oil for drizzling

Directions:

1. Roll out the pizza dough and place it on the French Door Air Fryer Oven trays.
2. Spread pizza sauce evenly over the dough, leaving a small border.
3. Arrange sliced mozzarella and tomatoes on top. Add fresh basil leaves.
4. Set the oven to the Pizza function at 400°F for 12-15 minutes, or until the crust is golden and cheese is melted.
5. Drizzle with olive oil, slice, and serve immediately.

Nutritional Value (Amount per Serving):

Calories: 513; Fat: 18.8; Carb: 62.02; Protein: 24.09

Whole Wheat Cinnamon Raisin Bread

Prep Time: 30 Minutes   Cook Time: 40 Minutes   Serves: 8

Ingredients:

- 2 cups whole wheat flour
- 1 cup all-purpose flour
- 1/4 cup honey
- 1 tablespoon active dry yeast
- 1 cup warm milk
- 1/4 cup unsalted butter, melted
- 1 cup raisins
- 1 teaspoon cinnamon

Directions:

1. Mix warm milk, honey, and yeast in a bowl. Let it sit for 10 minutes until frothy.
2. In a large bowl, combine flours, melted butter, raisins, and cinnamon. Add the yeast mixture and knead until smooth.
3. Divide the dough in half and shape into loaves. Place them on the French Door Air Fryer pans.
4. Set the oven to the Bake function at 350°F for 35-40 minutes, or until the bread is golden and sounds hollow when tapped.
5. Allow to cool before slicing.

Nutritional Value (Amount per Serving):

Calories: 247; Fat: 5.48; Carb: 44.64; Protein: 7.47

BBQ Chicken Naan Pizza

Prep Time: 25 Minutes   Cook Time: 18 Minutes   Serves: 4

Ingredients:

- 2 naan bread
- 1/2 cup BBQ sauce
- 1 cup cooked chicken, shredded
- 1 cup shredded mozzarella cheese
- 1/2 red onion, thinly sliced
- Fresh cilantro, chopped

Directions:

1. Place naan bread on the French Door Air Fryer Oven trays.
2. Spread BBQ sauce on each naan, then add shredded chicken, mozzarella, and red onion.
3. Set the oven to the Pizza function at 375°F for 15-18 minutes, or until the cheese is bubbly and golden.
4. Sprinkle with fresh cilantro before serving.

Nutritional Value (Amount per Serving):

Calories: 350; Fat: 16.89; Carb: 27.67; Protein: 21.72

Rosemary Olive Oil Flatbread

Prep Time: 20 Minutes   Cook Time: 12 Minutes   Serves: 6

Ingredients:

- 2 cups all-purpose flour
- 1 teaspoon salt
- 1 tablespoon fresh rosemary, chopped
- 3/4 cup warm water
- 1/4 cup olive oil
- 1/2 cup mixed olives, sliced

Directions:

1. In a bowl, mix flour, salt, and rosemary. Add warm water and olive oil, kneading until a smooth dough forms.
2. Divide the dough into small balls and roll them out into flatbreads.
3. Place the flatbreads on the French Door Air Fryer Oven trays, brush with olive oil, and sprinkle with sliced olives.
4. Set the oven to the Bake function at 400°F for 10-12 minutes, or until the flatbreads are golden and slightly crispy.
5. Serve warm and enjoy.

Nutritional Value (Amount per Serving):

Calories: 244; Fat: 10.62; Carb: 32.56; Protein: 4.41

Sun-Dried Tomato and Basil Focaccia

Prep Time: 25 Minutes   Cook Time: 30 Minutes   Serves: 6

Ingredients:

- 2 1/2 cups all-purpose flour
- 1 tablespoon sugar
- 1 tablespoon active dry yeast
- 1 cup warm water
- 3 tablespoons olive oil
- 1/4 cup sun-dried tomatoes, chopped
- 2 tablespoons fresh basil, chopped
- Salt and pepper to taste

Directions:

1. In a bowl, combine warm water, sugar, and yeast. Let it sit for 5 minutes until foamy.
2. In a large mixing bowl, combine flour, olive oil, sun-dried tomatoes, basil, salt, and pepper. Add the yeast mixture and sit it for 20 minutes, then knead until a soft dough forms.
3. Press the dough onto a greased baking tray of the French Door Air Fryer Oven.
4. Set the air fryer oven to the Bake function at 375°F for 25-30 minutes until the top is golden.
5. Slice and serve warm.

Nutritional Value (Amount per Serving):

Calories: 270; Fat: 7.5; Carb: 43.89; Protein: 6.68

Sausage and Pepperoni Stromboli

Prep Time: 30 Minutes   Cook Time: 20 Minutes   Serves: 8

Ingredients:

- 1 pound pizza dough
- 1/2 cup marinara sauce
- 1/2 pound Italian sausage, cooked and crumbled
- 1/2 cup pepperoni slices
- 1 cup shredded mozzarella cheese
- 1/2 cup bell peppers, thinly sliced

Directions:

1. Preheat the French Door Air Fryer Oven to the Pizza function at 375°F.
2. Roll out the pizza dough into a rectangle.
3. Spread marinara sauce on the dough, leaving an inch border around the edges.
4. Layer cooked sausage, pepperoni, mozzarella, and bell peppers.
5. Roll the dough tightly, seal the edges, and place in the Air Fryer Oven for 15-20 minutes until golden brown.

Nutritional Value (Amount per Serving):

Calories: 315; Fat: 13.72; Carb: 32.49; Protein: 15.22

Garlic Parmesan Pull-Apart Bread

Prep Time: 15 Minutes   Cook Time: 25 Minutes   Serves: 6

Ingredients:

- 1 loaf of Italian bread
- 1/2 cup unsalted butter, melted
- 3 cloves garlic, minced
- 1/4 cup fresh parsley, chopped
- 1/2 cup grated Parmesan cheese

Directions:

1. Preheat the French Door Air Fryer Oven to the Bake function at 375°F.
2. Slice the Italian bread into 1-inch cubes without cutting all the way through.
3. In a bowl, mix melted butter, minced garlic, chopped parsley, and grated Parmesan.
4. Gently open the slices of the bread and brush the mixture generously between each slice.

5. Place the bread in the Air Fryer Oven and bake for 20-25 minutes until the top is golden and crisp.

Nutritional Value (Amount per Serving):

Calories: 336; Fat: 15.28; Carb: 39.61; Protein: 9.81

Caprese Stuffed Garlic Bread

Prep Time: 20 Minutes   Cook Time: 15 Minutes   Serves: 4

Ingredients:

- 1 baguette
- 4 tablespoons unsalted butter, softened
- 3 cloves garlic, minced
- 1 cup cherry tomatoes, sliced
- 1 cup fresh mozzarella, sliced
- Fresh basil leaves for garnish
- Balsamic glaze for drizzling

Directions:

1. Preheat the French Door Air Fryer Oven to the Bake function at 375°F.
2. Slice the baguette in half lengthwise.
3. Mix softened butter and minced garlic, then spread it evenly on the cut sides of the baguette.
4. Layer sliced cherry tomatoes and fresh mozzarella on one half.
5. Place the baguette in the Air Fryer Oven for 12-15 minutes until the cheese is melted and bubbly.
6. Garnish with fresh basil leaves and drizzle with balsamic glaze before serving.

Nutritional Value (Amount per Serving):

Calories: 428; Fat: 10.53; Carb: 62.04; Protein: 22.09

Spinach and Feta Stuffed Flatbread

Prep Time: 25 Minutes   Cook Time: 20 Minutes   Serves: 6

Ingredients:

- 2 pieces of flatbread
- 1 cup frozen spinach, thawed and drained
- 1/2 cup feta cheese, crumbled
- 1/4 cup red onion, finely chopped
- 1/4 cup black olives, sliced
- Olive oil for brushing

Directions:

1. Preheat the French Door Air Fryer Oven to the Pizza function at 400°F.
2. Spread thawed spinach over the flatbreads.
3. Sprinkle crumbled feta, chopped red onion, and sliced black olives evenly.

4. Drizzle with olive oil and place in the Air Fryer Oven for 15-20 minutes until the edges are golden.
5. Slice and serve warm.

Nutritional Value (Amount per Serving):

Calories: 132; Fat: 9.05; Carb: 8.99; Protein: 4.45

Pesto Chicken Artichoke Pizza

Prep Time: 30 Minutes   Cook Time: 18 Minutes   Serves: 4

Ingredients:

- 1 pound pizza dough
- 1/2 cup pesto sauce
- 1 cup cooked chicken, shredded
- 1/2 cup artichoke hearts, chopped
- 1 cup shredded mozzarella cheese
- 1/4 cup Parmesan cheese, grated

Directions:

1. Roll out the pizza dough and place it on the tray/pan of the French Door Air Fryer Oven.
2. Spread pesto sauce evenly over the dough.
3. Add shredded chicken, chopped artichoke hearts, mozzarella, and Parmesan.
4. Set the air fryer oven to the Pizza function at 400°F for 15-18 minutes until the crust is golden and cheese is melted.
5. Slice and serve hot.

Nutritional Value (Amount per Serving):

Calories: 740; Fat: 41.49; Carb: 62.74; Protein: 30.02

Cheddar and Jalapeño Cornbread

Prep Time: 15 Minutes   Cook Time: 25 Minutes   Serves: 8

Ingredients:

- 1 1/2 cups cornmeal
- 1/2 cup all-purpose flour
- 1 teaspoon baking powder
- 1/2 teaspoon baking soda
- 1/2 teaspoon salt
- 1 1/4 cups buttermilk
- 2 large eggs
- 1/4 cup unsalted butter, melted
- 1 cup sharp cheddar cheese, shredded
- 2 jalapeños, seeded and diced

Directions:

1. Preheat the French Door Air Fryer Oven to the Bake function at 375°F.
2. In a bowl, combine cornmeal, flour, baking powder, baking soda, and salt.
3. In another bowl, whisk buttermilk, eggs, and melted butter.
4. Mix the wet and dry ingredients, then fold in shredded cheddar and diced

jalapeños.

5. Pour the batter into a greased baking dish and bake for 20-25 minutes until golden.

Nutritional Value (Amount per Serving):

Calories: 299; Fat: 14.08; Carb: 32.74; Protein: 10.36

Prosciutto and Fig Flatbread

Prep Time: 20 Minutes   Cook Time: 15 Minutes   Serves: 4

Ingredients:

- 2 pieces of flatbread
- 1/2 cup fig jam
- 4 ounces prosciutto
- 1 cup arugula
- Balsamic glaze for drizzling
- Shaved Parmesan for garnish

Directions:

1. Preheat the French Door Air Fryer Oven to the Pizza function at 400°F.
2. Spread fig jam evenly on the flatbreads.
3. Layer prosciutto on top and place the flatbreads in the Air Fryer Oven for 12-15 minutes until the edges are crisp.
4. Top with fresh arugula, drizzle with balsamic glaze, and garnish with shaved Parmesan before serving.

Nutritional Value (Amount per Serving):

Calories: 150; Fat: 2.86; Carb: 26.27; Protein: 6.39

Apple Cinnamon Pull-Apart Bread

Prep Time: 25 Minutes   Cook Time: 30 Minutes   Serves: 6

Ingredients:

- 1 pound pizza dough
- 2 apples, peeled and thinly sliced
- 1/4 cup brown sugar
- 1 teaspoon cinnamon
- 1/4 cup unsalted butter, melted
- Powdered sugar for dusting

Directions:

1. Roll out the pizza dough into a rectangle.
2. Mix sliced apples, brown sugar, and cinnamon in a bowl.
3. Spread the apple mixture evenly over the dough, then roll it up.
4. Cut the rolled dough into slices and place them in a pan the French Door Air Fryer Oven.
5. Drizzle melted butter over the top and bake using the Bake function at 375°F for 25-30 minutes until golden.
6. Dust with powdered sugar before serving.

Nutritional Value (Amount per Serving):

Calories: 367; Fat: 12.8; Carb: 57.39; Protein: 7.09

Buffalo Chicken Flatbread

Prep Time: 20 Minutes   Cook Time: 15 Minutes   Serves: 4

Ingredients:

- 2 pieces of flatbread
- 1 cup cooked chicken, shredded
- 1/4 cup buffalo sauce
- 1/2 cup blue cheese, crumbled
- 1/4 cup celery, thinly sliced
- Ranch dressing for drizzling

Directions:

1. Preheat the French Door Air Fryer Oven to the Pizza function at 400°F.
2. Toss shredded chicken in buffalo sauce.
3. Spread the buffalo chicken over the flatbreads and top with blue cheese.
4. Bake in the Air Fryer Oven for 12-15 minutes until the crust is crisp.
5. Garnish with sliced celery and drizzle with ranch dressing before serving.

Nutritional Value (Amount per Serving):

Calories: 319; Fat: 21.77; Carb: 18.49; Protein: 12.1

Cranberry Walnut Artisan Bread

Prep Time: 30 Minutes   Cook Time: 40 Minutes   Serves: 8

Ingredients:

- 3 cups bread flour
- 1 1/2 teaspoons salt
- 1/2 teaspoon active dry yeast
- 1 1/2 cups warm water
- 1/2 cup dried cranberries
- 1/2 cup chopped walnuts

Directions:

1. In a bowl, mix bread flour, salt, and yeast. Add warm water and sit it for 20 minutes, then knead until smooth.
2. Fold in dried cranberries and chopped walnuts.
3. Shape the dough into a round and place it in the French Door Air Fryer Oven.
4. Set the oven to the Bake function at 375°F for 35-40 minutes until the bread is golden and sounds hollow when tapped.
5. Cool before slicing.

Nutritional Value (Amount per Serving):

Calories: 228; Fat: 4.15; Carb: 40.19; Protein: 7.02

Mushroom and Truffle Oil Pizza

Prep Time: 25 Minutes   Cook Time: 18 Minutes   Serves: 4

Ingredients:

- 1 pound pizza dough
- 1/2 cup Alfredo sauce
- 1 1/2 cups mushrooms, sliced
- 1 cup fontina cheese, shredded
- Truffle oil for drizzling
- Fresh thyme for garnish

Directions:

1. Roll out the pizza dough and place it on the French Door Air Fryer Oven tray/pan.
2. Spread Alfredo sauce evenly over the dough.
3. Arrange sliced mushrooms on top and sprinkle with shredded fontina.
4. Set the oven to the Pizza function at 400°F for 15-18 minutes until the crust is golden.
5. Drizzle with truffle oil and garnish with fresh thyme before serving.

Nutritional Value (Amount per Serving):

Calories: 664; Fat: 35.52; Carb: 65; Protein: 21.3

Caramelized Onion and Goat Cheese Focaccia

Prep Time: 20 Minutes   Cook Time: 30 Minutes   Serves: 6

Ingredients:

- 2 1/2 cups all-purpose flour
- 1 tablespoon sugar
- 1 tablespoon active dry yeast
- 1 cup warm water
- 3 tablespoons olive oil
- 2 large onions, thinly sliced
- 1/2 cup goat cheese, crumbled
- Balsamic reduction for drizzling

Directions:

1. In a bowl, combine warm water, sugar, and yeast. Let it sit for 5 minutes until foamy.
2. In a large mixing bowl, combine flour, olive oil, and the yeast mixture. Knead until a soft dough forms.
3. Press the dough onto a greased baking tray of the French Door Air Fryer Oven.
4. In a pan, caramelize the thinly sliced onions.
5. Spread caramelized onions over the dough and sprinkle with crumbled goat cheese.
6. Set the oven to the Bake function at 375°F for 25-30 minutes until the top is golden.
7. Drizzle with balsamic reduction before serving.

Nutritional Value (Amount per Serving):

Calories: 360; Fat: 13.43; Carb: 47.7; Protein: 12.03

Sunflower Seed and Honey Wheat Bread

Prep Time: 25 Minutes   Cook Time: 40 Minutes   Serves: 8

Ingredients:

- 2 cups whole wheat flour
- 1 cup all-purpose flour
- 1 tablespoon active dry yeast
- 1 1/4 cups warm water
- 2 tablespoons honey
- 1/4 cup sunflower seeds
- 1 teaspoon salt

Directions:

1. In a bowl, mix warm water, honey, and yeast. Let it sit for 10 minutes until frothy.
2. In a large mixing bowl, combine whole wheat flour, all-purpose flour, sunflower seeds, and salt.
3. Add the yeast mixture and knead until a soft dough forms.
4. Shape the dough into a loaf and place it in the French Door Air Fryer Oven.
5. Set the oven to the Bake function at 375°F for 35-40 minutes until the bread is golden and sounds hollow when tapped.
6. Allow to cool before slicing.

Nutritional Value (Amount per Serving):

Calories: 205; Fat: 3.27; Carb: 39.33; Protein: 7.11

BBQ Pulled Pork Stuffed Pretzels

Prep Time: 30 Minutes   Cook Time: 25 Minutes   Serves: 6

Ingredients:

- 1 pound pizza dough
- 1 cup pulled pork, cooked
- 1/2 cup BBQ sauce
- 1 cup cheddar cheese, shredded
- 1/4 cup green onions, chopped
- Pretzel salt for sprinkling

Directions:

1. Preheat the French Door Air Fryer Oven to the Bake function at 375°F.
2. Roll out the pizza dough into a rectangle.
3. Mix pulled pork with BBQ sauce and spread it evenly over the dough.
4. Sprinkle shredded cheddar and chopped green onions.
5. Roll the dough into a log, cut it into pretzel-sized pieces, and place them in the Air Fryer Oven.
6. Bake for 20-25 minutes until the pretzels are golden.
7. Sprinkle with pretzel salt before serving.

Nutritional Value (Amount per Serving):

Calories: 335; Fat: 11.04; Carb: 42.74; Protein: 16.02

Chapter 7: Appetizers and Snacks

Loaded Sweet Potato Skins

Prep Time: 15 Minutes   Cook Time: 40-45 Minutes   Serves: 6

Ingredients:

- 3 medium-sized sweet potatoes
- 1 cup cooked and crumbled bacon
- 1 cup shredded cheddar cheese
- 1/2 cup sour cream
- 2 green onions, finely chopped
- Salt and pepper to taste

Directions:

1. Preheat the French Door Air Fryer Oven to 375°F using the Bake function.
2. Scrub sweet potatoes and pat dry. Pierce each potato with a fork and bake for 30 minutes using the Roast function.
3. Once cooled, cut sweet potatoes in half lengthwise. Scoop out the flesh, leaving a thin layer.
4. Set the oven to 400°F using the Air Fry function.
5. Place sweet potato skins in the air fryer basket, cook for 8-10 minutes until crispy.
6. Fill each skin with bacon and cheese, then air fry for an additional 5 minutes until the cheese is melted.
7. Top with sour cream, green onions, salt, and pepper before serving.

Nutritional Value (Amount per Serving):

Calories: 255; Fat: 12.79; Carb: 23.68; Protein: 11.35

Crispy Apple Chips

Prep Time: 15 Minutes   Cook Time: 4 Hours   Serves: 4

Ingredients:

- 4 large apples, cored and thinly sliced
- 1 tablespoon lemon juice
- 1 teaspoon ground cinnamon

Directions:

1. Toss apple slices with lemon juice to prevent browning.
2. Arrange the apple slices on the air fryer trays, ensuring they do not overlap.
3. Sprinkle cinnamon evenly over the apple slices.
4. Set the French Door Air Fryer Oven to the Dehydrate function at 135°F for 4 hours or until the apple chips are crispy.
5. Allow the chips to cool before serving.

Nutritional Value (Amount per Serving):

Calories: 139; Fat: 0.89; Carb: 35.14; Protein: 0.41

Spicy Kale Chips

Prep Time: 10 Minutes   Cook Time: 3 Hours   Serves: 3

Ingredients:

- 1 bunch of kale, stems removed and torn into bite-sized pieces
- 2 tablespoons olive oil
- 1 teaspoon chili powder
- 1/2 teaspoon garlic powder
- Salt to taste

Directions:

1. In a large bowl, massage kale with olive oil until well coated.
2. Sprinkle chili powder, garlic powder, and salt over the kale, tossing to ensure even coating.
3. Arrange the seasoned kale pieces on the air fryer trays, leaving space between them.
4. Set the French Door Air Fryer Oven to the Dehydrate function at 125°F for 3 hours or until the kale chips are crispy.
5. Allow the chips to cool before serving.

Nutritional Value (Amount per Serving):

Calories: 86; Fat: 9.18; Carb: 1.3; Protein: 0.44

BBQ Chicken Quesadillas

Prep Time: 15 Minutes   Cook Time: 10 Minutes   Serves: 4

Ingredients:

- 2 cups cooked and shredded chicken
- 1/2 cup BBQ sauce
- 1 cup shredded cheddar cheese
- 1/2 cup diced red onion
- 4 large flour tortillas

Directions:

1. Preheat the Air Fryer Oven to 375°F using the Bake function.
2. In a bowl, combine shredded chicken with BBQ sauce.
3. Lay out the tortillas, spread chicken mixture, cheese, and red onions on half of each tortilla.
4. Fold the tortillas in half and air fry for 10 minutes, flipping halfway, until golden and crispy.

Nutritional Value (Amount per Serving):

Calories: 539; Fat: 32.27; Carb: 35.61; Protein: 25.84

Spinach and Artichoke Stuffed Mushrooms

Prep Time: 20 Minutes   Cook Time: 15 Minutes   Serves: 5

Ingredients:

- 20 large white mushrooms, stems removed
- 1 cup frozen chopped spinach, thawed and drained
- 1/2 cup canned artichoke hearts, finely chopped
- 1/2 cup cream cheese, softened
- 1/4 cup grated Parmesan cheese
- Salt and pepper to taste

Directions:

1. Preheat the Air Fryer Oven to 375°F using the Bake function.
2. In a bowl, mix spinach, artichoke hearts, cream cheese, Parmesan, salt, and pepper.
3. Stuff each mushroom cap with the mixture and place on the air fryer tray.
4. Air fry for 12-15 minutes until mushrooms are tender and filling is golden.
5. Serve hot.

Nutritional Value (Amount per Serving):

Calories: 132; Fat: 8.79; Carb: 8.4; Protein: 7.81

Buffalo Cauliflower Bites

Prep Time: 15 Minutes   Cook Time: 25 Minutes   Serves: 4

Ingredients:

- 1 head cauliflower, cut into florets
- 1 cup all-purpose flour
- 1 cup milk
- 1 cup buffalo sauce
- 1/4 cup melted butter
- 1 teaspoon garlic powder
- 1 teaspoon onion powder

Directions:

1. Preheat the Air Fryer Oven to 400°F using the Air Fry function.
2. In a bowl, whisk together flour, milk, garlic powder, and onion powder to create a batter.
3. Dip cauliflower florets into the batter and place them on the air fryer tray/pan.
4. Air fry for 15 minutes, tossing halfway through.
5. In a separate bowl, mix buffalo sauce and melted butter.
6. Toss the cooked cauliflower in the sauce and air fry for an additional 5 minutes.

Nutritional Value (Amount per Serving):

Calories: 397; Fat: 14.47; Carb: 60.25; Protein: 7.32

Stuffed Jalapeño Poppers

Prep Time: 25 Minutes   Cook Time: 20 Minutes   Serves: 5

Ingredients:

- 10 large jalapeños, halved and seeds removed
- 1 cup cream cheese, softened
- 1 cup shredded cheddar cheese
- 1 cup cooked and crumbled sausage
- 1 teaspoon smoked paprika
- Salt and pepper to taste

Directions:

1. Preheat the Air Fryer Oven to 375°F using the air fry function.
2. In a bowl, mix cream cheese, cheddar cheese, sausage, smoked paprika, salt, and pepper.
3. Stuff each jalapeño half with the mixture.
4. Arrange the stuffed jalapeños on the air fryer tray/pan and air fry for 15-20 minutes until golden.

Nutritional Value (Amount per Serving):

Calories: 268; Fat: 21.53; Carb: 8.78; Protein: 11.95

Sweet and Spicy Bacon-Wrapped Dates

Prep Time: 20 Minutes   Cook Time: 25 Minutes   Serves: 6

Ingredients:

- 18 Medjool dates, pitted
- 9 slices bacon, cut in half
- 1/2 cup goat cheese
- 1/4 cup honey
- 1 teaspoon cayenne pepper (optional)

Directions:

1. Preheat the Air Fryer Oven to 375°F using the air fry function.
2. Stuff each date with a teaspoon of goat cheese.
3. Wrap each stuffed date with half a slice of bacon.
4. Secure with toothpicks and place on the air fryer tray/pan.
5. Air fry for 20-25 minutes until the bacon is crispy.
6. Drizzle with honey and sprinkle with cayenne pepper if desired before serving.

Nutritional Value (Amount per Serving):

Calories: 477; Fat: 21.41; Carb: 66.48; Protein: 11.35

Broiled Crab-Stuffed Mushrooms

Prep Time: 25 Minutes   Cook Time: 15 Minutes   Serves: 5

Ingredients:

- 20 large mushrooms, stems removed
- 1 lb lump crab meat, drained
- 1/2 cup cream cheese, softened
- 1/4 cup mayonnaise
- 1/4 cup grated Parmesan cheese
- 2 cloves garlic, minced
- 1 tablespoon fresh lemon juice
- Salt and pepper to taste

Directions:

1. Preheat the French Door Air Fryer Oven at 350°F using the broil function.
2. In a bowl, mix crab meat, cream cheese, mayonnaise, Parmesan, garlic, lemon juice, salt, and pepper.
3. Stuff each mushroom cap with the mixture.
4. Place the mushrooms on a tray and broil for 10-12 minutes until the tops are golden.

Nutritional Value (Amount per Serving):

Calories: 441; Fat: 15.11; Carb: 41.13; Protein: 41.52

Keep Warm Spinach and Artichoke Dip

Prep Time: 10 Minutes   Cook Time: 30 Minutes   Serves: 8

Ingredients:

- 1 cup frozen chopped spinach, thawed and drained
- 1 cup canned artichoke hearts, chopped
- 1 cup cream cheese, softened
- 1/2 cup mayonnaise
- 1/2 cup sour cream
- 1 cup shredded mozzarella cheese
- 1/2 cup grated Parmesan cheese
- 2 cloves garlic, minced
- Salt and pepper to taste
- Tortilla chips or bread for dipping

Directions:

1. Set the Keep Warm function in the French Door Air Fryer Oven to 250°F.
2. In a bowl, combine spinach, artichokes, cream cheese, mayonnaise, sour

cream, mozzarella, Parmesan, garlic, salt, and pepper.
3. Transfer the mixture to an oven-safe dish.
4. Place the dish in the French Door Air Fryer Oven and keep warm for 30 minutes.
5. Serve with tortilla chips or bread for dipping.

Nutritional Value (Amount per Serving):

Calories: 239; Fat: 17.56; Carb: 10.01; Protein: 11.54

Slow Cooker Sweet and Sour Meatballs

Prep Time: 15 Minutes   Cook Time: 4 Hours   Serves: 6

Ingredients:

- 1 lb frozen meatballs
- 1 cup pineapple chunks
- 1 bell pepper, diced
- 1/2 cup ketchup
- 1/4 cup soy sauce
- 1/4 cup brown sugar
- 1/4 cup rice vinegar
- 1 teaspoon garlic powder
- 1/2 teaspoon ginger powder
- Green onions for garnish
- Cooked rice for serving

Directions:

1. In baking dish, combine meatballs, pineapple chunks, bell pepper, ketchup, soy sauce, brown sugar, rice vinegar, garlic powder, and ginger powder.
2. Set the Slow Cook function at 300°F in the French Door Air Fryer Oven and cook for 4 hours.
3. Stir occasionally during cooking.
4. Garnish with green onions and serve over cooked rice.

Nutritional Value (Amount per Serving):

Calories: 364; Fat: 18.89; Carb: 38.1; Protein: 12.72

Rotisserie Buffalo Cauliflower Bites

Prep Time: 20 Minutes   Cook Time: 40 Minutes   Serves: 4

Ingredients:

- 1 head cauliflower, cut into florets
- 1/2 cup buffalo sauce
- 1/4 cup melted butter
- 1 teaspoon garlic powder
- 1 teaspoon onion powder
- Salt and pepper to taste
- Blue cheese dressing for dipping

Directions:

1. Preheat the Rotisserie function in the French Door Air Fryer Oven to

375°F.

2. In a bowl, combine cauliflower florets, buffalo sauce, melted butter, garlic powder, onion powder, salt, and pepper.
3. Skewer the cauliflower on the rotisserie rod.
4. Rotisserie for 30-40 minutes until cauliflower is tender.
5. Serve with blue cheese dressing for dipping.

Nutritional Value (Amount per Serving):

Calories: 223; Fat: 15.59; Carb: 20.32; Protein: 2.2

Stuffed Bell Pepper Poppers

Prep Time: 25 Minutes   Cook Time: 15 Minutes   Serves: 6

Ingredients:

- 12 mini bell peppers, halved and seeds removed
- 1 cup cooked quinoa
- 1/2 cup black beans, drained and rinsed
- 1/2 cup corn kernels
- 1 cup shredded cheddar cheese
- 1 teaspoon cumin
- 1/2 teaspoon chili powder
- Salt and pepper to taste
- Fresh cilantro for garnish

Directions:

1. Preheat the Broil function in the French Door Air Fryer Oven to 400°F.
2. In a bowl, mix quinoa, black beans, corn, cheese, cumin, chili powder, salt, and pepper.
3. Stuff each bell pepper half with the mixture.
4. Place the peppers on a tray/pan and broil for 12-15 minutes or until cheese is bubbly.
5. Garnish with fresh cilantro before serving.

Nutritional Value (Amount per Serving):

Calories: 152; Fat: 3.41; Carb: 24.37; Protein: 8.44

Slow Cooker Buffalo Chicken Dip

Prep Time: 10 Minutes   Cook Time: 2 Hours   Serves: 8

Ingredients:

- 2 cups cooked and shredded chicken

- 1 cup cream cheese, softened
- 1/2 cup buffalo sauce
- 1/2 cup ranch dressing
- 1 cup shredded cheddar cheese
- 1/2 cup crumbled blue cheese
- 2 green onions, chopped
- Tortilla chips or celery sticks for dipping

Directions:

1. In the air fryer oven, combine shredded chicken, cream cheese, buffalo sauce, ranch dressing, cheddar cheese, blue cheese, and green onions.
2. Set the Slow Cook function to 370°F. and cook for 2 hours.
3. Stir occasionally during cooking.
4. Once hot and bubbly, switch to Keep Warm function.
5. Serve with tortilla chips or celery sticks.

Nutritional Value (Amount per Serving):

Calories: 395; Fat: 31.73; Carb: 14.82; Protein: 12.9

Rotisserie Bacon-Wrapped Asparagus

Prep Time: 15 Minutes   Cook Time: 20 Minutes   Serves: 4

Ingredients:

- 1 lb asparagus spears, trimmed
- 8 slices bacon
- Olive oil
- Salt and pepper to taste
- Lemon wedges for serving

Directions:

1. Preheat the Rotisserie function of the French Door Air Fryer Oven at 375°F.
2. Wrap each asparagus spear with a slice of bacon.
3. Secure with toothpicks and brush with olive oil.
4. Skewer the asparagus bundles on the rotisserie rod.
5. Rotisserie for 15-20 minutes or until bacon is crispy.
6. Season with salt and pepper, serve with lemon wedges.

Nutritional Value (Amount per Serving):

Calories: 304; Fat: 27.71; Carb: 6.72; Protein: 9.28

Dehydrated Veggie Chips Assortment

Prep Time: 15 Minutes   Cook Time: 4 Hours   Serves: 6

Ingredients:

- 2 sweet potatoes, thinly sliced
- 2 beets, thinly sliced
- 2 zucchinis, thinly sliced
- 2 tablespoons olive oil
- 1 teaspoon garlic powder
- 1 teaspoon paprika
- Salt and pepper to taste

Directions:

1. Preheat the Dehydrate function in the French Door Air Fryer Oven to 125°F.
2. In separate bowls, toss sweet potatoes, beets, and zucchinis with olive oil, garlic powder, paprika, salt, and pepper.
3. Arrange the slices on the air fryer oven trays/pans.
4. Dehydrate for 4 hours or until the veggie chips are crispy.

Nutritional Value (Amount per Serving):

Calories: 107; Fat: 4.79; Carb: 16.23; Protein: 1.7

Rotisserie Garlic Parmesan Corn on the Cob

Prep Time: 15 Minutes   Cook Time: 25 Minutes   Serves: 6

Ingredients:

- 6 ears of corn, husked
- 1/2 cup unsalted butter, melted
- 1/2 cup grated Parmesan cheese
- 3 cloves garlic, minced
- 1 tablespoon chopped fresh parsley
- Salt and black pepper to taste
- Lime wedges for serving

Directions:

1. Preheat the Rotisserie function in the French Door Air Fryer Oven to 400°F.
2. Brush each ear of corn with melted butter.
3. In a bowl, mix Parmesan cheese, minced garlic, parsley, salt, and black pepper.
4. Roll each corn cob in the Parmesan mixture, ensuring it's well-coated.
5. Skewer the corn on the rotisserie rod.
6. Rotisserie for 20-25 minutes or until the corn is tender and lightly browned.
7. Serve with lime wedges on the side.

Nutritional Value (Amount per Serving):

Calories: 258; Fat: 14.33; Carb: 30.22; Protein: 7.88

Dehydrated Spiced Mango Slices

Prep Time: 10 Minutes   Cook Time: 6 Hours   Serves: 4

Ingredients:

- 2 large mangoes, peeled and thinly sliced
- 1 tablespoon chili powder
- 1 teaspoon cayenne pepper
- 1 tablespoon honey

Directions:

1. Preheat the Dehydrate function in the French Door Air Fryer Oven to 135°F.
2. In a bowl, toss mango slices with chili powder, cayenne pepper, and honey.
3. Arrange the slices on the air fryer trays/pans.
4. Dehydrate for 6 hours or until the mango slices are chewy and slightly crispy.

Nutritional Value (Amount per Serving):

Calories: 124; Fat: 1; Carb: 30.74; Protein: 1.72

Chapter 8: Desserts

Triple Chocolate Brownie Delight

Prep Time: 15 Minutes   Cook Time: 30 Minutes   Serves: 8-10

Ingredients:

- 1 cup unsalted butter, melted
- 2 cups granulated sugar
- 4 large eggs
- 1 teaspoon vanilla extract
- 1 cup all-purpose flour
- 1/2 cup cocoa powder
- 1/2 teaspoon baking powder
- 1/2 teaspoon salt
- 1 cup white chocolate chips
- 1 cup milk chocolate chips
- 1 cup dark chocolate chips

Directions:

1. Preheat the French Door Air Fryer Oven to 350°F.
2. In a large bowl, whisk together melted butter, sugar, eggs, and vanilla extract until well combined.
3. In a separate bowl, sift together flour, cocoa powder, baking powder, and salt. Add this dry mixture to the wet ingredients and mix until just combined.
4. Fold in white, milk, and dark chocolate chips until evenly distributed.
5. Pour the batter onto a greased baking pan and place it on the Air Fryer Oven tray.
6. Bake for 25-30 minutes or until a toothpick inserted into the center comes out with a few moist crumbs.
7. Allow the brownies to cool before slicing.
8. Serve and enjoy!

Nutritional Value (Amount per Serving):

Calories: 436; Fat: 23.69; Carb: 52.73; Protein: 6.46

Mixed Berry Crumble

Prep Time: 20 Minutes   Cook Time: 40 Minutes   Serves: 6-8

Ingredients:

- 4 cups mixed berries (strawberries, blueberries, raspberries)
- 1/2 cup granulated sugar
- 2 tablespoons cornstarch
- 1 tablespoon lemon juice
- 1 cup rolled oats
- 1/2 cup all-purpose flour
- 1/2 cup brown sugar
- 1/2 cup unsalted butter, softened

- 1/2 teaspoon cinnamon
- Pinch of salt

Directions:

1. Preheat the Air Fryer Oven to 375°F.
2. In a large bowl, combine mixed berries, granulated sugar, cornstarch, and lemon juice. Toss until the berries are evenly coated.
3. In a separate bowl, mix rolled oats, flour, brown sugar, softened butter, cinnamon, and salt until crumbly.
4. Spread the berry mixture in a baking dish and sprinkle the crumble topping evenly over the berries.
5. Place the dish on the Air Fryer tray and bake for 30-35 minutes or until the topping is golden brown and the berries are bubbly.
6. Allow the crumble to cool slightly before serving.
7. Serve with a scoop of vanilla ice cream if desired.

Nutritional Value (Amount per Serving):

Calories: 430; Fat: 18.79; Carb: 66.37; Protein: 5.48

Cinnamon Sugar Donuts

Prep Time: 15 Minutes   Cook Time: 10 Minutes   Serves: 6-8

Ingredients:

- 1 cup all-purpose flour
- 1/2 cup granulated sugar
- 1 teaspoon baking powder
- 1/2 teaspoon ground cinnamon
- 1/2 cup milk
- 1 large egg
- 2 tablespoons unsalted butter, melted
- 1 teaspoon vanilla extract
- 1/4 cup unsalted butter, melted
- 1/2 cup granulated sugar
- 1 teaspoon ground cinnamon

Directions:

1. Preheat the Air Fryer Oven to 350°F.
2. In a bowl, whisk together flour, sugar, baking powder, and cinnamon.
3. In another bowl, whisk together milk, egg, melted butter, and vanilla extract.
4. Add the wet ingredients to the dry ingredients, stirring until just combined.
5. Spoon the batter into a greased donut pan, filling each cavity about two-thirds full.
6. Bake in the Air Fryer Oven for 8-10 minutes or until the donuts are lightly golden.
7. While the donuts are still warm, dip each one in melted butter and then roll in the cinnamon-sugar mixture until coated.

Calories: 203; Fat: 8.01; Carb: 29.66; Protein: 3.2

Apple-Pecan Bread Pudding

Prep Time: 20 Minutes   Cook Time: 45 Minutes   Serves: 6-8

Ingredients:

- 6 cups cubed stale bread
- 2 medium apples, peeled and diced
- 1/2 cup chopped pecans
- 4 large eggs
- 2 cups whole milk
- 1/2 cup granulated sugar
- 1/4 cup brown sugar
- 1 teaspoon vanilla extract
- 1 teaspoon ground cinnamon
- 1/2 teaspoon nutmeg
- Pinch of salt

Directions:

1. Preheat the Air Fryer Oven to 350°F.
2. In a large bowl, combine cubed bread, diced apples, and chopped pecans.
3. In another bowl, whisk together eggs, milk, granulated sugar, brown sugar, vanilla extract, cinnamon, nutmeg, and salt.
4. Pour the egg mixture over the bread mixture and gently toss until the bread is evenly coated.
5. Transfer the mixture to a greased baking dish and place it on the Air Fryer tray.
6. Bake for 40-45 minutes or until the top is golden brown and the pudding is set.
7. Allow the bread pudding to cool slightly before serving.
8. Serve with a drizzle of caramel sauce if desired.

Nutritional Value (Amount per Serving):

Calories: 311; Fat: 10.96; Carb: 47.62; Protein: 7.08

Strawberry Shortcake Skewers

Prep Time: 20 Minutes   Cook Time: 10 Minutes   Serves: 4-6

Ingredients:

- 1 pound fresh strawberries, hulled and halved
- 1 package store-bought pound cake, cut into bite-sized cubes
- 1 cup whipped cream
- 1/4 cup powdered sugar
- 1 teaspoon vanilla extract
- Wooden skewers

Directions:

1. Preheat the Air Fryer Oven to 375°F.
2. In a small bowl, mix whipped cream, powdered sugar, and vanilla extract until stiff peaks form. Set aside.
3. Thread alternating strawberry halves and pound cake cubes onto wooden skewers, creating strawberry shortcake skewers.
4. Place the skewers on the Air Fryer tray, ensuring they are not touching each other.
5. Air fry for 8-10 minutes or until the pound cake is golden brown and the strawberries are slightly softened.
6. Remove the skewers from the Air Fryer tray and let them cool for a few minutes.
7. Serve the strawberry shortcake skewers with a dollop of whipped cream on the side for dipping.

Nutritional Value (Amount per Serving):

Calories: 512; Fat: 13.51; Carb: 96.17; Protein: 2.08

Molten Lava Chocolate Cake

Prep Time: 15 Minutes   Cook Time: 12 Minutes   Serves: 4-6

Ingredients:

- 1 cup semi-sweet chocolate chips
- 1/2 cup unsalted butter
- 1/4 cup all-purpose flour
- 1/2 cup powdered sugar
- 3 large eggs
- 1 teaspoon vanilla extract
- Pinch of salt
- Optional: Vanilla ice cream for serving

Directions:

1. Preheat the Air Fryer Oven to 375°F using the Bake function.
2. In a microwave-safe bowl, melt chocolate chips and butter together. Stir until smooth.
3. In a separate bowl, whisk together flour, powdered sugar, eggs, vanilla extract, and a pinch of salt.
4. Gradually fold the melted chocolate mixture into the batter until well combined.
5. Divide the batter among ramekins and place them in the Air Fryer Oven.
6. Bake for 10-12 minutes or until the edges are set but the center is still gooey.

7. Carefully remove from the Air Fryer Oven, let it cool for a minute, and serve. Optionally, top with vanilla ice cream.

Nutritional Value (Amount per Serving):

Calories: 346; Fat: 23.33; Carb: 32.76; Protein: 4.75

Grilled Peach and Honey Parfait

Prep Time: 10 Minutes   Cook Time: 8 Minutes   Serves: 4-6

Ingredients:

- 4 ripe peaches, halved and pitted
- 2 tablespoons honey
- 1 cup Greek yogurt
- 1/2 cup granola
- Mint leaves for garnish

Directions:

1. Preheat the Air Fryer Oven to 400°F using the Grill function.
2. Brush peach halves with honey and grill for 4 minutes on each side.
3. Once grilled, dice the peaches into bite-sized pieces.
4. In serving glasses, layer grilled peaches, Greek yogurt, and granola.
5. Repeat the layers and finish with a drizzle of honey and a garnish of mint leaves.

Nutritional Value (Amount per Serving):

Calories: 187; Fat: 4.92; Carb: 34.21; Protein: 4.14

Slow Cooked Apple Cinnamon Pudding

Prep Time: 15 Minutes   Cook Time: 2 Hours   Serves: 6-8

Ingredients:

- 6 cups peeled and sliced apples
- 1/2 cup granulated sugar
- 1 teaspoon ground cinnamon
- 1/4 teaspoon ground nutmeg
- 1 cup water
- 2 cups dry bread cubes
- 1/2 cup raisins
- 2 tablespoons unsalted butter, melted
- Whipped cream for serving

Directions:

1. In a bowl, combine sliced apples, sugar, cinnamon, and nutmeg. Toss to coat.
2. Transfer the apple mixture to the tray/pan of the Air Fryer Oven.
3. Pour water over the apples and stir to combine.
4. In a separate bowl, mix bread cubes, raisins, and melted butter. Sprinkle this mixture over the apples.

5. Cover and cook on the Slow Cook function for 2 hours at 370°F.
6. Serve warm, topped with a dollop of whipped cream.

Nutritional Value (Amount per Serving):

Calories: 135; Fat: 3.63; Carb: 25.85; Protein: 1.41

Dehydrated Citrus Fruit Chips

Prep Time: 10 Minutes   Cook Time: 4 Hours   Serves: 4-6

Ingredients:

- Assorted citrus fruits (oranges, lemons, limes, grapefruits)
- 1 tablespoon honey (optional)

Directions:

1. Thinly slice citrus fruits using a mandolin or sharp knife.
2. If desired, brush each slice with a thin layer of honey for added sweetness.
3. Arrange the slices on the trays/pans of the Air Fryer Oven.
4. Set the Air Fryer Oven to the Dehydrate function at 135°F and dehydrate for 4 hours or until the fruits are dry and crispy.
5. Allow the citrus chips to cool before serving. Enjoy as a healthy, natural snack.

Nutritional Value (Amount per Serving):

Calories: 96; Fat: 0.05; Carb: 24.18; Protein: 0.63

Air-Fried S'mores Empanadas

Prep Time: 20 Minutes   Cook Time: 10 Minutes   Serves: 4-6

Ingredients:

- 1 package refrigerated pie crusts
- 1 cup mini marshmallows
- 1/2 cup chocolate chips
- 1/4 cup crushed graham crackers
- 1 egg (beaten, for egg wash)
- Powdered sugar (for dusting)

Directions:

1. Roll out the pie crusts and cut them into circles.
2. In the center of each circle, place a few mini marshmallows, chocolate chips, and a sprinkle of crushed graham crackers.
3. Fold the circles in half, sealing the edges with a fork.
4. Brush each empanada with beaten egg for a golden finish.
5. Air fry in the Air Fryer Oven at 375°F for 8-10 minutes or until golden brown.
6. Dust with powdered sugar before serving.

Nutritional Value (Amount per Serving):

Calories: 327; Fat: 17.59; Carb: 38.14; Protein: 4.15

Broiled Pineapple with Cinnamon Sugar

Prep Time: 15 Minutes   Cook Time: 8 Minutes   Serves: 4-6

Ingredients:

- 1 pineapple, peeled and cored
- 2 tablespoons melted butter
- 2 tablespoons brown sugar
- 1 teaspoon ground cinnamon
- Vanilla ice cream for serving

Directions:

1. Slice the pineapple into rings.
2. In a small bowl, mix melted butter, brown sugar, and cinnamon.
3. Brush both sides of each pineapple slice with the butter mixture.
4. Place the slices on the pan of the Air Fryer Oven using the Broil function.
5. Broil for 4 minutes on each side or until the edges are caramelized.
6. Serve warm with a scoop of vanilla ice cream.

Nutritional Value (Amount per Serving):

Calories: 127; Fat: 5.11; Carb: 21.47; Protein: 1.05

Baked Cinnamon Sugar Pretzel Bites

Prep Time: 30 Minutes   Cook Time: 12 Minutes   Serves: 4-6

Ingredients:

- 1 pound pizza dough
- 1/4 cup baking soda
- 1 cup hot water
- 2 tablespoons unsalted butter, melted
- 1/2 cup granulated sugar
- 1 tablespoon ground cinnamon

Directions:

1. Preheat the Air Fryer Oven to 375°F using the Bake function.
2. Roll out the pizza dough and cut it into bite-sized pieces.
3. In a small bowl, dissolve baking soda in hot water.
4. Dip each dough piece into the baking soda mixture and place them on the baking tray.
5. Bake for 10-12 minutes or until golden brown.
6. Brush with melted butter and toss in a mixture of sugar and cinnamon while still warm.

Nutritional Value (Amount per Serving):

Calories: 368; Fat: 12.16; Carb: 57.25; Protein: 8.17

Grilled Banana Split

Prep Time: 15 Minutes   Cook Time: 6 Minutes   Serves: 4-6

Ingredients:

- 4 bananas, peeled and halved lengthwise
- 1/2 cup chocolate chips
- 1/2 cup chopped nuts (walnuts or almonds)
- Vanilla ice cream
- Whipped cream
- Maraschino cherries

Directions:

1. Preheat the Air Fryer Oven to 400°F using the Grill function.
2. Place banana halves on the grill pan and cook for 3 minutes on each side.
3. Remove from the pan and sprinkle chocolate chips over the warm bananas.
4. Allow the chocolate to melt slightly, then sprinkle with chopped nuts.
5. Serve the grilled bananas with scoops of vanilla ice cream, whipped cream, and a cherry on top.

Nutritional Value (Amount per Serving):

Calories: 519; Fat: 19.25; Carb: 90.64; Protein: 6.12

Dehydrated Fruit Roll-Ups

Prep Time: 15 Minutes   Cook Time: 4 Hours   Serves: 4-6

Ingredients:

- 4 cups mixed berries (strawberries, blueberries, raspberries)
- 2 tablespoons honey
- 1 tablespoon lemon juice

Directions:

1. In a blender, puree the mixed berries, honey, and lemon juice until smooth.
2. Pour the mixture onto the trays of the Air Fryer Oven.
3. Set the Air Fryer Oven to the Dehydrate function at 135°F and dehydrate for 4 hours or until the fruit leather is no longer sticky.
4. Cut the fruit leather into strips and roll them up.
5. Store in an airtight container.

Nutritional Value (Amount per Serving):

Calories: 551; Fat: 25.01; Carb: 79.2; Protein: 4.7

Slow Cooked Bread Pudding with Rum Sauce

Prep Time: 20 Minutes   Cook Time: 3 Hours   Serves: 6-8

Ingredients:

- 6 cups cubed stale bread
- 1 cup raisins
- 4 cups whole milk
- 4 large eggs
- 1 cup granulated sugar
- 1/4 cup unsalted butter, melted
- 1 teaspoon vanilla extract
- 1 teaspoon ground cinnamon
- 1/2 teaspoon nutmeg
- Pinch of salt
- 1/2 cup unsalted butter
- 1 cup brown sugar
- 1/4 cup dark rum

Directions:

1. In a large bowl, combine cubed bread and raisins.
2. In another bowl, whisk together milk, eggs, sugar, melted butter, vanilla extract, cinnamon, nutmeg, and salt.
3. Pour the egg mixture over the bread mixture and stir until well combined.
4. Transfer the mixture to baking dish in the Air Fryer Oven.
5. Cover and cook on the Slow Cook function for 3 hours.
6. In the last 15 minutes, prepare the rum sauce by melting butter in a saucepan, then adding brown sugar and rum. Simmer until slightly thickened.
7. Drizzle the bread pudding with rum sauce before serving.

Nutritional Value (Amount per Serving):

Calories: 554; Fat: 21.15; Carb: 78.77; Protein: 9.19

Broiled Berry Bruschetta

Prep Time: 15 Minutes   Cook Time: 8 Minutes   Serves: 4-6

Ingredients:

- 1 French baguette, sliced
- 1/2 cup mascarpone cheese
- 1 cup mixed berries (strawberries, blueberries, raspberries)
- 2 tablespoons honey
- Fresh mint leaves for garnish

Directions:

1. Preheat the Air Fryer Oven to 400°F using the Broil function.
2. Arrange baguette slices on the tray/pan and broil for 2-3 minutes on each side or until golden brown.
3. Spread mascarpone cheese on each baguette slice.

4. In a bowl, mix berries and honey.
5. Spoon the berry mixture over the mascarpone.
6. Garnish with fresh mint leaves before serving.

Nutritional Value (Amount per Serving):

Calories: 357; Fat: 13.21; Carb: 50.39; Protein: 10.35

Roasted Almond Cherry Galette

Prep Time: 25 Minutes   Cook Time: 25 Minutes   Serves: 6-8

Ingredients:

- 1 pre-made pie crust
- 1 cup almond flour
- 1/2 cup granulated sugar
- 1/2 cup unsalted butter, softened
- 1 teaspoon almond extract
- 2 cups fresh or frozen cherries, pitted
- Sliced almonds for garnish
- Powdered sugar for dusting

Directions:

1. Preheat the Air Fryer Oven to 375°F using the Bake function.
2. Roll out the pie crust on a baking sheet.
3. In a bowl, mix almond flour, sugar, softened butter, and almond extract to form a crumbly mixture.
4. Spread the almond mixture evenly over the pie crust, leaving a border around the edges.
5. Arrange the cherries on top of the almond mixture.
6. Fold the edges of the pie crust over the cherries, creating a rustic galette.
7. Air fry for 20-25 minutes or until the crust is golden brown.
8. Garnish with sliced almonds and dust with powdered sugar before serving.

Nutritional Value (Amount per Serving):

Calories: 328; Fat: 18.36; Carb: 39.28; Protein: 3.25

Balsamic Strawberry & Basil Bruschetta

Prep Time: 15 Minutes   Cook Time: 6 Minutes   Serves: 4-6

Ingredients:

- 1 French baguette, sliced
- 2 cups fresh strawberries, diced
- 2 tablespoons balsamic glaze
- 1 tablespoon honey
- Fresh basil leaves, chopped

- Whipped ricotta cheese for spreading

Directions:

1. Preheat the Air Fryer Oven to 400°F using the Broil function.
2. Arrange baguette slices on the tray/pan and broil for 2-3 minutes on each side or until golden brown.
3. In a bowl, mix diced strawberries, balsamic glaze, honey, and chopped basil.
4. Spread whipped ricotta on each baguette slice.
5. Spoon the strawberry mixture on top.
6. Serve immediately.

Nutritional Value (Amount per Serving):

Calories: 249; Fat: 7; Carb: 39.34; Protein: 8.54

Crispy Cinnamon Sugar Plantain Chips

Prep Time: 15 Minutes   Cook Time: 3 Hours   Serves: 4-6

Ingredients:

- 4 ripe plantains
- 2 tablespoons melted coconut oil
- 1/4 cup granulated sugar
- 1 teaspoon ground cinnamon

Directions:

1. Peel and thinly slice the plantains.
2. In a bowl, toss plantain slices with melted coconut oil.
3. Arrange the slices on the trays/pans of the Air Fryer Oven.
4. Set the Air Fryer Oven to the Dehydrate function at 135°F and dehydrate for 3 hours or until the chips are crispy.
5. In a separate bowl, mix sugar and cinnamon. Toss the dehydrated plantain chips in the mixture until coated.
6. Allow the chips to cool before serving.

Nutritional Value (Amount per Serving):

Calories: 288; Fat: 5.79; Carb: 64.85; Protein: 1.52

APPENDIX RECIPE INDEX

Made in the USA
Las Vegas, NV
14 October 2024

96766560R00063